Advocacy from A to Z

In today's educational climate, advocacy is a critical part of any teacher or leader's job. *Advocacy from A to Z* unpacks the difficult task of understanding the movers and shakers—including teachers, parents, the union, legislatures, and policy makers—that impact your school, affect your students, and shape policy. Organized into 26 chapters—one for each letter of the alphabet—this book provides school-based examples and specific strategies needed to be a successful advocate for education. Advocacy begins at the local level, and the newest book in the *A to Z* series helps educational leaders navigate, plan, and shape their message to the right people at the right time. Now you can find your voice and become an active advocate to help your students succeed.

Dr. Robert Blackburn has been a lifelong educator. After teaching in public schools and earning his doctorate, he became a professor at Louisiana College and Gardner-Webb University. Before his retirement, he was active in the area of health education, particularly in the movement for Smoke Free Schools in North Carolina and drug abuse prevention. He received the National Association of Local Boards of Health's (NALBOH) Everett I. Hageman Award for his outstanding leadership on a local board of health, as well as commitment to and enthusiasm for local public health.

Dr. Barbara R. Blackburn is the bestselling author of 17 books and is a sought-after consultant. She was an award-winning professor at Winthrop University and has taught students of all ages. Barbara was named as one of the Top 30 Education Gurus in the world for 2017 by Global Gurus.

Dr. Ronald Williamson is Professor of Educational Leadership at Eastern Michigan University. He is a former principal, central office administrator, and executive director of the National Middle School Association (now AMLE).

Other Eye on Education Books Available From Routledge

(www.routledge.com/eyeoneducation)

Rigor in Your School: A Toolkit for Leaders, 2nd Edition
Ronald Williamson and Barbara R. Blackburn

Leading Schools in an Era of Declining Resources
J. Howard Johnston and Ronald Williamson

The School Leader's Guide to Social Media
Ronald Williamson and J. Howard Johnston

Get Organized! Time Management for School Leaders, 2nd Edition
Frank Buck

Rigor in Your Classroom: A Toolkit for Teachers
Barbara R. Blackburn

Motivating Struggling Learners: 10 Ways to Build Student Success
Barbara R. Blackburn

Leading Learning for ELL Students: Strategies for Success
Catherine Beck and Heidi Pace

Leadership in America's Best Urban Schools
Joseph F. Johnson, Jr., Cynthia L. Uline, and Lynne G. Perez

Keeping the Leadership in Instructional Leadership: Developing Your Practice
Linda L. Carrier

The Educational Leader's Guide for School Scheduling: Strategies Addressing Grades K–12
Elliot Y. Merenbloom and Barbara A. Kalina

Understanding Key Education Issues
Matthew Lynch

Response to Intervention and Continuous School Improvement: How to Design, Implement, Monitor, and Evaluate a Schoolwide Prevention System, 2nd Edition
Victoria L. Bernhardt and Connie L. Hébert

A to Z *Series*

The Principalship from A to Z, 2nd Edition
Ronald Williamson and Barbara R. Blackburn

Classroom Instruction from A to Z, 2nd Edition
Barbara R. Blackburn

Classroom Motivation from A to Z: How to Engage Your Students in Learning
Barbara R. Blackburn

Literacy from A to Z
Barbara R. Blackburn

Advocacy from A to Z

Robert Blackburn
Barbara R. Blackburn
and Ronald Williamson

Taylor & Francis Group
NEW YORK AND LONDON

First published 2018
by Routledge
711 Third Avenue, New York, NY 10017

and by Routledge
2 Park Square, Milton Park, Abingdon, Oxon, OX14 4RN

Routledge is an imprint of the Taylor & Francis Group, an informa business

© 2018 Taylor & Francis

The right of Robert Blackburn, Barbara R. Blackburn, and Ronald Williamson to be identified as authors of this work has been asserted by them in accordance with sections 77 and 78 of the Copyright, Designs and Patents Act 1988.

All rights reserved. No part of this book may be reprinted or reproduced or utilized in any form or by any electronic, mechanical, or other means, now known or hereafter invented, including photocopying and recording, or in any information storage or retrieval system, without permission in writing from the publishers.

Trademark notice: Product or corporate names may be trademarks or registered trademarks, and are used only for identification and explanation without intent to infringe.

Library of Congress Cataloging-in-Publication Data
A catalog record for this book has been requested

ISBN: 978-1-138-12550-6 (hbk)
ISBN: 978-1-138-12551-3 (pbk)
ISBN: 978-1-315-64747-0 (ebk)

Typeset in Palatino
by Apex CoVantage, LLC

Bob—To Rose, my loving wife of over 60 years, for her unwavering support and encouragement. Her dedication to our family allowed me to be an advocate for educators and public health.

Barbara—To my dad and coauthor of this book. I've always dreamed of writing with the person I admire the most. Thank you for creating this book with me.

Ron—To my wife Marsha, our children, and grandchildren for their love, support, and understanding of my passion for helping school leaders improve America's schools.

Contents

eResources xi
Acknowledgments xiii
Meet the Authors xv
Introduction xvii

A   Advocacy: What and Why? 1
B   Building Blocks of Lobbying 7
C   Communication Skills 13
D   Designing an Advocacy Plan 19
E   Engaging Through Technology 25
F   Framing Your Message 29
G   Gaining Support with Limited Resources 35
H   Handling the Media 41
I   Internal and External Stakeholders 47
J   Juggling Information 51
K   Keys to Social Media 57
L   Local Advocacy Is Foundational 63
M   Motivating Those Around You 69
N   Networking 75
O   Overcoming Objections 81
P   Public Relations 101 87
Q   Quality Relationships 93
R   Resistance to Change 101
S   Successful Negotiations 109
T   Time, Friend or Foe? 115
U   Up-to-Date on the Issues 121

V	Vision: Personal and Shared	127
W	Working with Local, State, and National Governance	133
X	X Factor: Pitfalls to Avoid	141
Y	Your Turn	147
Z	Zeroing in on the Essentials	153

Bibliography 159
Appendix 163

eResources

Many of the tools in this book can be downloaded and printed for classroom use. You can access these downloads by visiting the book product page on our website: www.routledge.com/9781138125513. Then click on the "eResources" tab and select the files. They will begin downloading to your computer.

- Interacting with Your School Board (C). 17
- Sample Advocacy Plan (D) 22
- Tips for Talking with the Media (H). 44
- 11 Ways Your School Can Use Twitter (K). 60
- Creating Your Key Communicator Network (N). 79
- Helpful Ideas for Communicating When
  Conflict Is Present (R). 107
- Sample Vision Letter (V) 130

Acknowledgments

- Our families and friends for their unwavering support throughout this project. Thank you for your patience when we shared ideas and when we asked for advice on drafts. Most importantly, you kept us grounded and in touch with the work needed to improve America's schools.
- Colleagues in the Department of Leadership and Counseling at Eastern Michigan University. You are a source of great support, encouragement, and creative thinking.
- Colleagues at the American Heart Association and the Association of North Carolina Boards of Health (ANCBH).
- Dr. Frank Buck, author of *Get Organized! Time Management Strategies for School Leaders*, for his writings on organizing information and managing time.
- The hundreds of teachers and school leaders we've met in our classrooms and in our work with schools. We applaud your energy, your commitment, and your dedication to the youth of America. But, most importantly, we value your questions, your comments, and your unwavering inquisitiveness.
- All the educators and other stakeholders who advocate for their issues on a regular basis. They truly make a difference in education.
- Heather Jarrow, our editor. We appreciate the opportunity to share this information.
- To the reviewers, Kara Chism and Karen Hickman, thanks for your suggestions, which helped us clarify and refine the content.
- John Maloney, thank you for a wonderful cover design.
- To Fred Dahl and Apex CoVantage, thanks for the great jobs you did in copyediting and page makeup.

Meet the Authors

Dr. Robert Blackburn (Bob) has been a lifelong educator. After teaching in public schools and earning his doctorate, he became a professor at Louisiana College and Gardner-Webb University. Before his retirement, he was active in the area of health education, particularly in the movement for Smoke Free Schools in North Carolina and drug abuse prevention.

He received the National Association of Local Boards of Health's (NALBOH) Everett I. Hageman Award, which is awarded to a board of health member who has demonstrated outstanding leadership on a local board of health, as well as commitment to and enthusiasm for local public health. He has been recognized by the Cleveland County Commissioners for contributions to public health. He has received two Bronze Medallions from the American Health Association (AHA)-North Carolina (NC) for his work as an AHA volunteer; the Leadership Award from the NC Tri-Agency Task Force for outstanding leadership in the Smoke-Free Class of 2000; and honor awards from state, district, and national AAHPERD (American Association of Health, Physical Education, Recreation, and Dance) organizations. He is a fellow of the North American Society of HPERSD Professionals. In the spring of 2008, he was presented the inaugural Dr. Robert Blackburn Advocacy Award by the North Carolina American Heart Association.

Since his retirement, he has been active in advocacy work in the public health arena. Nationally, he has served on the Department of Health and Human Services Secretary's Council on Health Promotion and Disease Prevention, was president of the Association for the Advancement of Health Education, president of the Society of Association Management, president of the National Association of Local Boards of Health, and president of the Foundation for the Advancement of Health Education. He has made over 100 presentations on health, advocacy, and health policy. He chaired the Joint Committee on National Health Education Standards, which published its work in 1995.

On the state level, he has been president of the Association of North Carolina Boards of Health, a member of Healthy Carolinians Task Force; vice chair of the NC Local Health Department Accreditation Board; a member of four accreditation site visit teams, the NC Task Force on Obesity, the Eat

Smart Move More Leadership Team, the Division of Public Health, and the NC Institute of Public Health Assessment Team; and chair of the North Carolina School Health Advisory Committee.

Barbara R. Blackburn, PhD, has dedicated her life to raising the level of rigor and motivation for professional educators and students alike. What differentiates Barbara's 17 books are her easily executable concrete examples based on decades of experience as a teacher, professor, and consultant. Barbara's dedication to education was inspired in her early years by her parents, Bob and Rose. Her father's doctorate and lifetime career as a professor taught her the importance of professional training. Her mother's career as school secretary shaped Barbara's appreciation of the effort that all staff play in the education of every child.

Barbara has taught early childhood, elementary, middle, and high school students and has served as an educational consultant for three publishing companies. She holds a master's degree in school administration and was certified as a teacher and school principal in North Carolina. She received her doctorate in Curriculum and Teaching from the University of North Carolina at Greensboro. In 2006, she received the award for Outstanding Junior Professor at Winthrop University. She left her position at the University of North Carolina at Charlotte to write and speak full-time.

Recently named one of the Top 30 Education Gurus in the world, she speaks at state and national conferences, as well as regularly presenting workshops for teachers and administrators in elementary, middle, and high schools. Her workshops are lively and engaging and filled with practical information. For more information or to schedule professional development, please contact her at her website: www.barbarablackburnonline.com.

Ronald Williamson is a professor of educational leadership at Eastern Michigan University. He previously taught at the University of North Carolina at Greensboro and was a public school administrator in Michigan. Ron has also served as the executive director of the National Middle School Association (now AMLE) and as president of the National Forum to Accelerate Middle Grades Reform. In both roles, he advocated for sound programs serving middle-grade students at both the federal and the state levels. His work as an advocate informs this book.

Ron is the author of numerous articles and books on leadership and effective leadership practices. He provided direct services to several large urban districts as a leadership coach, funded by the Edna McConnell Clark Foundation and the Galef Institute of Los Angeles. He currently works with the Oregon GEAR UP program to provide research services and leadership support to more than 50 rural middle and high schools throughout Oregon.

Introduction

In today's educational climate, advocacy is a critical part of any teacher or leader's job. We have to advocate to our school board for our school's needs, advocate to business leaders for support of the school, advocate to parents to help us enable their children to be successful, and advocate to local, state, and national policy makers to provide funding for our issues.

This book came from feedback from the readers of our previous books, *Rigorous Schools and Classrooms: Leading the Way* and *Rigor in Your School: A Toolkit for Leaders*. In both of those books, Ron and Barbara wrote about the COMPASS model for school leadership: Culture, Ownership and Shared Vision, Managing Data, Professional Development, Advocacy, Shared Accountability, and Structures to Sustain Success.

In those books, readers particularly like the approach to advocacy because teachers and leaders do not believe they are equipped to be advocates with all of today's pressures. So Ron and Barbara approached Barbara's dad, Robert Blackburn. As a lifelong advocate for education and health, he assisted with the earlier books and had broad experience and knowledge in the area of advocacy.

Together, we drafted a list of issues related to advocacy and talked with teachers, leaders, and other stakeholders to focus on the most helpful topics. You'll find very specific strategies, along with school-based examples. Additionally, reflective questions at the end of each chapter allow you to process the information presented and plan your next steps. Finally, in the appendix, we've provided a list of educational websites that focus on advocacy. These can help you as you move forward in your journey to being an advocate.

This book is part of our A to Z series (*Classroom Instruction from A to Z, Literacy from A to Z, Classroom Motivation from A to Z,* and *The Principalship from A to Z*). They are designed to cover a wide range of topics within a specific subject. There is no specific order to the chapters. Scan the table of contents and choose where you would like to start based on your needs. We hope you will use these strategies to be a stronger advocate for education, whether you are a teacher advocating to a parent, a teacher advocating for additional support for a student with special needs, a leader advocating for a business to provide volunteers for your school, a teacher or leader advocating to a school board for approval to pilot a new program, or a teacher or leader advocating to local, state, or government officials for a particular position that will benefit your school. As you employ these strategies, we hope you will provide feedback to Barbara (bcgroup@gmail.com) so we can better support teachers and leaders across the nation.

A

Advocacy: What and Why?

Human progress is neither automatic nor inevitable. . . . Every step toward the goal of justice requires sacrifice, suffering, and struggle; the tireless exertions and passionate concern of dedicated individuals.

—Martin Luther King, Jr.

Everyone is an advocate, whether you recognize it or not. We advocate for our favorite teams or political candidates, and, of course, we advocate for our schools and the resources and programs vital to the success of our students. For a leader, advocacy is one of your most important roles.

Advocacy is what you do when you are actively supporting a cause, such as expanding the emphasis on technology in your school. It is often compared to public relations. But advocacy is quite different, as we'll discuss throughout the book. When leaders advocate for their program, they are committed to providing information to stakeholder groups that will build support for their vision of increased technology use. They recognize the importance of building networks and alliances that will support their efforts.

Advocacy is a way to systematically press for change. It is also the foundation of our democracy and a process that allows ordinary people to shape and influence policy at all levels. Identifying priorities, crafting a strategy, taking action, and achieving results are critical steps to finding one's voice, making oneself heard, and shaping one's future.

Why Should I Be an Advocate?

There are five major reasons to become an advocate.

Reasons to Become an Advocate

1. Decisions will be made whether you are involved or not.
2. You have important grassroots knowledge that decision makers need to know.
3. Decisions will impact you, whether you are involved or not.
4. Advocacy starts with one, and that one is you.
5. You are an advocate, either active or passive.

First, understand that decisions will be made about issues important to your school, whether you are involved or not. Have you ever felt as though decisions affecting your work were made by other people and that you didn't get to share your thoughts? If you've ever felt that way, then you should become an advocate.

You also have specific knowledge, based on your work in the trenches, that is valuable to those making decisions. Too often, decision makers make choices without having an understanding of how those choices impact teachers and educational leaders. Therefore, we need to share our knowledge.

As you have probably experienced, decisions impact you with or without your input. Barbara has always said, "People who make decisions about education should spend at least a week in the classroom. That would give them a better perspective." Or, as the old adage says, "You can't really understand the experience of others until you've walked a mile in their shoes." Your thinking and suggestions can inform a decision in ways that will positively impact student learning.

Next, advocacy starts with one person, and that one person is you. If everyone waits for the next person to be an advocate, there will be no advocates for education. We often think one person can't make a difference, but that's not true. Let's look at classic examples from history—times when one vote made a difference.

How Important Is One Vote?

In 1649, **one vote** caused Charles I of England to be executed.

In 1776, **one vote** gave America the English language instead of German.

In 1845, **one vote** brought Texas into the Union.

In 1923, **one vote** gave the leadership of the Nazi Party to Adolph Hitler.

In 1960, John F. Kennedy won the presidency by an average of less than **one vote** per precinct in the United States.

Finally, realize that you are an advocate, whether you want to be or not. You advocate for your issues, either actively or passively. Passively, if you choose not to share your perspective with decision makers, then your silence says you agree with them. The only question is do you want to advocate for your position actively or let the decision be made without your input?

Characteristics of an Effective Advocate

Once you decide you are an advocate, you want to be an effective one. There are eight characteristics of an effective advocate.

Eight Characteristics of an Effective Advocate

An effective advocate:

1. Always listens and learns.
2. Has a deliberate focus on long-term goals.
3. Values support from others.
4. Is open to different ways to share their message.
5. Is committed to partners with different views, as well as like-minded individuals.
6. Is able to look at and respond to positions in an issue.
7. Has the tenacity to bounce back from negative responses.
8. Engages the public and stakeholders.

Always Listens and Learns

Effective advocates listen to their audience and learn from them. Too often, we are so focused on sharing our message that we forget to listen. Without listening, we can't adjust as we learn about our audience's needs.

Deliberate Focus on Long-Term Goals

You'll also need a focus on your long-term goals. It's easy to become caught up in the immediate situation and lose recognition of the long-term impact. In one district where we worked, there was tension between the staff of two high schools about programs and resources when the district moved to a small learning communities model. Rather than grasp the importance of these communities for connecting students and teachers, the focus was on facilities, supplies, and materials. The local news media reported on the tension, and it undermined the district's efforts to improve the learning environment for students.

Values Support From Others

Third, it's important not to limit your perspective but be open to different points of view. For example, your legislator does not schedule a time to meet with you. Instead, he refers you to his aide who specializes in education. Although you may feel as though this is a step down, the support from a key aide can be invaluable when the legislator is seeking advice from his staff. Recognize that you need support from a variety of stakeholders and people who influence opinion.

Openness to Different Ways to Share Your Message

Although we should always have a plan to share our message, we should be open to modifying our methods. For example, when meeting with a legislator, we may have a scheduled 15-minute meeting, for which we prepare. But when we arrive at our scheduled time, we are told that she has a conflict but that you may walk with her to a meeting, which will be about two minutes. You'll need to adjust the way you share your message.

Commitment to Partners with Different Views, as Well as Like-Minded Individuals

To accomplish your goals, you will need to partner with those who agree with you *and* those who may not. That may sound contradictory, but if you don't find ways to partner with those who disagree with you, you won't accomplish your goals.

Ability to Look at and Respond to All Positions in an Issue

Next, you'll need to assess the varying positions in an issue, so that you can respond appropriately. It's not enough to simply look at your own perspective, which may be limited. If you plan to accomplish your goal and gain support from your stakeholders, you'll need to understand their perspectives in addition to yours. Otherwise, you can't address their needs.

Tenacity to Bounce Back From Negative Responses

Are you tenacious enough to cope with the negative responses you are likely to encounter? As you advocate for an issue, you will receive negative responses. This doesn't mean you will never accomplish your goals, but it does mean you will need to recover from a negative response to continue to advocate for your issues.

Engages the Public and Stakeholders

Finally, an effective advocate engages the public and stakeholders. If we are generally disengaged from others, we won't get our message across. Engaging those around us means being involved with them. Whether that is by participating in clubs or other organizations or by responding to blogs from possible audiences, engagement heightens your opportunity to be a successful advocate. Community partnerships and the relationships that emerge from those partnerships provide a critical avenue for advocacy.

Final Thoughts

Becoming an advocate is an exciting part of your job, whether you are a teacher, leader, superintendent, parent, or school board member. As an advocate, you can make a difference by creating and impacting positive change. Apply the characteristics of effective advocacy, and watch what you can accomplish.

Final Reflection Questions

What challenge do you face in this particular area of advocacy?

What was the most important thing you learned in this chapter?

How can you apply that lesson in your own situation?

In six months, if you look back on this learning, what would you like to have accomplished?

B

Building Blocks of Lobbying

I want to make it clear that the lobbying sector does an important job. It is very useful to the government to hear the views of a broad range of groups to make sure we get the best.

—Andrew Lansley

What is the difference between advocacy and lobbying? What skills are needed to be an effective lobbyist without crossing the line to becoming an annoyance?

Throughout this book, we'll focus on the broad concept of advocacy. Sometimes advocacy is mistaken for lobbying. Although they are similar and lobbying is a form of advocacy, there are key differences.

Lobbying typically focuses on influencing legislation at the state or national level. Advocacy, on the other hand, is a much broader concept, encompassing activities that might or might not include lobbying. Think of the two this way: Lobbying always involves advocacy, but advocacy does not always involve lobbying.

Here's an example that helps to illustrate the difference. A principal can advocate for her school by talking with local businesspeople about partnerships in support of school programs. It might be support for a reading enrichment initiative or internships for students in vocational education programs. In this case, the principal is advocating.

The same principal is a member of her state's professional organization for elementary principals. She decides to travel to the state capital, along with other principals, to meet with legislators to talk about increased funding for supplies and professional development by describing how those funds would be used. While at the capital, the principal is lobbying.

Differences Between Advocacy and Lobbying

Advocacy	Lobbying
Focus on educating about a specific issue	Attempt to influence specific legislation
No limit to the amount you can do	May be restricted to a percentage of your budget
All efforts aimed at having influence on an issue	One aspect of advocacy
Aimed at several stakeholders both within and outside the government	Aimed specifically at legislators and government officials
Arguing your case with anyone who will listen	Petitioning government

How Do I Know If I'm Lobbying Instead of Advocating?

While being an advocate, it is possible to move into some lobbying activities. In fact, tax-exempt, 501(c)(3) organizations may engage in lobbying activities as long as they don't do too much. If you are a member of an advocacy group, how do you balance the two roles?

According to the IRS, organizations or groups may "conduct educational meetings, prepare and distribute educational materials, or otherwise consider public policy issues in an educational manner without jeopardizing their tax-exempt status." In other words, advocacy groups can lobby for their cause as long as they keep their focus on educating people about policy issues.

The Effective Lobbyist

Since a lobbyist is also an advocate, an effective lobbyist incorporates the characteristics of an effective advocate, discussed in Chapter A: Advocacy: What and Why? However, other characteristics are key to effective lobbying.

Characteristics of the Effective Lobbyist

- Comprehensive knowledge of issues and process
- Knows elected officials and staff
- Effective communicator
- Commitment to partnership
- Constant communication
- Balances competing priorities
- Takes time for little things

Comprehensive Knowledge of Issues and Process

Effective lobbyists have a comprehensive knowledge of the legislative and appropriation processes. Both processes are intricate and require that you understand the ins and outs. If you don't understand the processes, it's nearly impossible to be successful. For example, you should know when during the legislative year bills get introduced, or you should understand how committee hearings work.

Knows Elected Officials

Lobbyists also need to know their elected officials, as well as their staff and their gatekeepers. A meeting with the official is essential, but you want to be more than a casual acquaintance. You want the visit to help you develop a relationship. Often, these relationships mean that you are seen as trustworthy and someone who can be relied upon for good, solid information.

You must also know the legislator's staff and their gatekeepers. When Bob went to Washington to visit elected officials on "lobby" days for a professional association, it was apparent that time with officials was at a premium. His first visit with a senator lasted for five minutes before the official was called to the Senate floor for a vote. He did refer Bob to a staff member who handled education issues. The staff member gave Bob 30 minutes for a full discussion of his issue. This meeting opened the door for future meetings, emails, and calls. Know your elected officials, as well as their staffs.

Effective Communicator

To be an effective communicator, a lobbyist must have a grasp of the total issue, which includes all sides of the issue. The ability to understand the varying aspects of an issue while still lobbying for your desired outcome is important. Effective communication for a lobbyist also includes presenting the issue without exaggerating and using local needs and stories to support your points.

Commitment to Partnership

Lobbying requires working with those on both sides of the aisle or issue. You'll need to partner not only with like-minded individuals but also with those who differ with you. You may not always agree, but you can come to consensus at times. Without support that goes beyond those who agree with you, you may not accomplish your goals. Partnering through collaboration is an essential component for effective lobbying.

Constant Communication

Communication is a two-way street, but effective lobbyists stay in constant communication with elected officials and their staffs, without being a nuisance. In the next section in this chapter, we'll look at 15 ways to keep in touch with elected officials.

Balances Competing Priorities

Many priorities demand a lobbyist's attention. The key to being an effective lobbyist is the ability to balance those demands.

Take Time for Little Things

Along with balancing competing priorities, effective lobbyists take time to process what is happening and to reflect on their progress, strengths, and challenges. They use this reflection to plan for the future. Finally, an effective lobbyist never forgets to say thank you, whether it is verbally or in writing.

15 Ways to Keep in Touch with Elected Officials

As just discussed, it's important to stay in regular communication with elected officials and their staffs, without negatively impacting the relationship. Amy Showalter of the American Heart Association provides *105 Ways to Keep in Touch with Your Elected Officials All Year*. Let's look at 15 of them.

15 Ways to Keep in Touch with Elected Officials

1. Write a letter to the editor of your local paper or to the paper's online blog, commending your legislature. Send a copy to the representative.
2. Post commentary on an Internet chat room acknowledging your lawmaker for his actions. Take a screen shot and email it to him.
3. Invite the lawmaker to speak at a community or professional group of which you are a member.
4. Offer to assist the lawmaker in customizing the presentation for the group.
5. Invite the legislator to your school for a tour to informally meet your faculty and staff. Ask those she meets to send thank-you notes to her.
6. Offer to contribute information on one of your areas of expertise for your legislator's upcoming column or email newsletter.
7. Write a note recognizing your lawmaker's efforts when you find that a legislative initiative that he actively championed has failed. It's common to receive words of congratulations when legislation is passed. Only sincere supporters are with representatives when they fall short.
8. Deliver or email a fact sheet on your school or district to your legislator. Include the impact you have on the community.
9. Conduct a monthly Web search for references to your legislator and forward the information to him or her.
10. Review the legislator's website. Find something of use and compliment her and her staff on the site.
11. Deliver any financial contributions you make to a candidate in person.
12. Attend an event where the opposing candidate is speaking, and take notes. Be objective and report just the facts. Give this information to the candidate or his staff.
13. Email pictures from the campaign trail to the lawmaker's staff for inclusion on the legislator's campaign website.
14. Send a note of congratulations or condolences after the election.
15. Send a note to the staff for helping you with a legislative issue.

Final Thoughts

As an advocate, your efforts may shift into lobbying. If so, you'll want to follow the guidelines discussed here and put your skills as an advocate to work to effectively influence elected officials.

Final Reflection Questions

What challenge do you face in this particular area of advocacy?

What was the most important thing you learned in this chapter?

How can you apply that lesson in your own situation?

In six months, if you look back on this learning, what would you like to have accomplished?

C

Communication Skills

The art of communication is the language of leadership.

—James Humes

Communication is central to your role as an advocate. If you can't communicate effectively, your message will never be heard. There are 10 principles of effective communication.

10 Principles of Effective Communication

1. Conciseness and consistency matter.
2. Open with your key point.
3. Match to your agenda.
4. Make it coherent.
5. Understand your audience.
6. Name your objective or desired action.
7. Courtesy rules.
8. Ask questions.
9. Tell a story.
10. Empathy helps.

10 Principles of Effective Communication

Follow these principles to make all your communications more effective.

Conciseness and Consistency Matter

It's important to have a concise message. Oftentimes, your listeners are busy, and they do not have a tremendous amount of time to give you. If you take too much time, they will either move on or tune out. Additionally, be consistent in your message. If you send unclear messages that are not consistent, you will confuse your audience.

Open with Your Key Point

We live in a busy world, and your audience will be busy. So start your verbal or written message with your key point. We will discuss this more in Chapter F: Framing Your Message, but don't bury your lead. When you are advocating an issue, begin with the most important thing you have to say. This way, if your listener does interrupt you, you will still have communicated your main point.

Match to Your Agenda

Next, be sure your message matches your agenda. You may be thinking this is common sense, but you might be surprised how often this does not occur. For example, we heard one principal discuss safety. Her goal was to convince the superintendent and cabinet to improve lighting in the parking lot and around the exterior of the building. But in her one-page fact sheet (see Chapter F: Framing Your Message), she never stated that as her goal. Instead, she simply shared information about the importance of school safety without focusing on her agenda. The decision makers were left with information but without a clear idea of what the principal wanted.

Make It Coherent

Similarly, you want to have a coherent message. If you stray off topic, you will lose your audience. Unfortunately, it's too easy to do this. A lack of focus can undermine your advocacy efforts. Notice in the following example that the topic moves away from the main idea. By the end of the talk, listeners are unsure as to what they are being asked to do?

Principal Advocating to a Local Rotary Group That They Support a New Math Initiative by Volunteering to Tutor Students (Given 5 Minutes by the Group)

> I'm very excited to share with you our new math initiative. We know it will result in higher test grades. It is one of the newest programs available, and there is a lot of research that shows it will work. We've studied it for over a year and know it works. Many of our teachers visited classrooms to see it. We will need your help to find people who will tutor students. This is part of our bigger program, which is to help students learn in all subject areas. Our reading program has increased test scores by 20% in four years, and you can tell our students are more confident readers. We've also implemented a science program that includes a focus on problem solving. I hope you will consider supporting us in our efforts to help all students to learn.

Understand Your Audience

As you craft your message, you'll want to understand your audience. As you interact with different stakeholders, you will find that each of them has different needs, goals, and prior experiences related to your agenda. Once you discover where they are coming from, you can tailor your message to them and improve your chances of being effective.

Name Your Objective or Desired Action

As you are delivering your message, be sure to ask for help with your objective or for a specific action. If you only present material, stakeholders are left with information but no idea what they're being asked to do. That's nice, but what do you want them to do with that information?

Issue	Desired Objective/Action
Desire to increase literacy instruction in all content areas	Additional funding for materials
Crumbling sidewalk outside school entrance	Funding from upcoming bond issue
Smaller class size at primary grades	Additional teachers

Courtesy Rules

As you communicate with stakeholders and influencers, courtesy should be at the forefront. We don't always see courtesy used in the advocacy process, but if you want to accomplish your goals, you will make more progress if you are considerate. This includes not only your words but also your nonverbal communication.

Nonverbal communication is particularly important. The wordless symbols we send can reinforce or negate our communication. Nonverbal signals can be positive if used correctly, or they can send a message that contradicts our advocacy efforts. Types of nonverbal communication include facial expressions, body movements and posture, gestures, touch, eye contact, space, and voice. A related impression that has become problematic in recent years is attention. If we care more about our cell phones than our meeting, it's likely that your audience will tune you out.

Ask Questions

Another important concept is to ask questions while you are delivering your message. People are more responsive when you talk with them, not at them. Part of effectively asking questions is listening. You should listen just as much as you talk. Asking questions is one way to have a conversation rather than simply stating information. The use of open-ended inquiry questions promotes dialogue.

Sample Questions to Use During an Advocacy Conversation

> I'm interested. What thoughts do you have on the issue?
> What thoughts do you have about how others might respond?
> How might you support this issue?

Tell a Story

As you are sharing information, tell a story that supports your ideas. Stories are personal, and people remember stories longer than they remember facts. If possible, you want to tell a firsthand account of a story, something that happened to you or that you experienced. However, secondhand stories can also be effective. Perhaps you can explain a personal experience someone else shared with you, such as how this issue will impact a child in your school. The point is that stories are effective, particularly if they tug at the heartstrings.

Empathy Helps

Finally, be empathetic with your audience. By showing that you understand where they are coming from, they will be more likely to listen to you. For example, you may be advocating for more money for career/technical education. You might want to speak with local business leaders or business groups like the Chamber of Commerce. Be sensitive to the local tax rate but at the same time stress how good career/technical education programs can provide skilled workers and lower training costs for new employees. In other words, turn it into a win-win for both business owners and the schools.

Communicating with Your School Board

Let's look at how those tips can play out in a school setting. Following are strategies to communicate with your school board. Consider how these approaches utilize the information we described earlier in the chapter.

Interacting with Your School Board

- Identify a parent or community spokesperson to help deliver your message to the board.
- Frame the importance of rigor in your opening statement. Link it to board goals and how students will be successful once they leave your school.
- Describe your plan in such a way that the board can see the link between your overall school improvement efforts and their goals.
- Share examples of your work to illustrate the impact. It can be very helpful to highlight the effect of greater rigor on one or more students.
- Give recognition to the individuals who have contributed to your success. It is a time for you to be modest and allow others to be recognized.
- Conclude your presentation by aligning your vision of improved rigor with the board's vision for the district.

Final Thoughts

Effectively communicating your message, whether verbally or nonverbally, whether on social media or through traditional media, is essential to your role as an advocate. Communication is a skill that can be learned, and you can improve your communication with practice.

Final Reflection Questions

What challenge do you face in this particular area of advocacy?

What was the most important thing you learned in this chapter?

How can you apply that lesson in your own situation?

In six months, if you look back on this learning, what would you like to have accomplished?

D

Designing an Advocacy Plan

Productivity is never an accident. It is always the result of a commitment to excellence, intelligent planning, and focused effort.

—Paul J. Meyer

Advocacy may seem like an intimidating idea. But, as we have said, it is an essential role for all leaders. Central to your success as an advocate is to develop an advocacy plan that will help you clarify your issue and articulate ways to build support.

Crafting an advocacy plan includes several distinct steps. First and foremost is to be clear about the issue. Be as specific as you can about what you want to achieve. For example, your focus may be expanding the literacy skills of your students.

Then you need to identify goals and accompanying strategies, to learn about your allies and opponents, as well as those who might emerge as allies or opponents, and to develop advocacy strategies and identify opportunities to impact their thinking. Finally, you need to implement your plan and monitor its results. These six steps will guide you in designing an advocacy plan.

Designing an Advocacy Plan

Step 1:	Describe the issue.
Step 2:	Identify current strengths and challenges.
Step 3:	Identify expected allies and opponents.
Step 4:	Be clear about your goals and objectives.
Step 5:	Develop and implement strategies.
Step 6:	Monitor and adjust.

Designing an Advocacy Plan
Step 1: Describe the Issue

Research and identify the issues, in written form, that you want to accomplish.

Written plans often help you clarify your thinking. They also help maintain your focus when you're tempted to stray from your plans. Identifying the issue may include parts or even all of your school's mission statement.

Step 2: Identify Current Strengths and Challenges

Second, identify current strengths and weaknesses. Use advisory groups to help develop this perspective. They can help you assess your current efforts, as well what is and is not working. Additionally, gather information about currently available resources to round out your planning. This will include what you have in terms of people, organization, money, facilities, and allies. By analyzing your resources, you will obtain a better picture of your strengths and weaknesses.

Step 3: Identify Expected Allies and Opponents

It is important to know the "who" in terms of community support and opposition. Targets of change may be either institutions, groups, individuals, or "hybrids," that is, people who could switch from one side to the other. You will want to invest time listening to all sides in order to plan your approach. It is likely that each group will have different needs for information, and thus you may need to develop different approaches for each of them.

Step 4: Be Clear About Your Goals and Objectives

Next, be clear about your goals and objectives. You should have long-term, intermediate, and short-term goals. Long-term goals are what you want to accomplish over an extended period of time. Intermediate goals move you forward toward your long-range goals, and short-term goals are achievable immediately and set the stage for more successes.

One strategy for setting goals is to use SMART+C goals: Specific, Measurable, Achievable, Relevant, Timed, *and* Challenging.

SMART+C

Specific—The more specific, the better the plan will be.

Measurable—Put your goals in measurable terms.

Achievable—Set realistic goals that your group can achieve.

Relevant—Your goals must be relevant to your mission and goals.

Timed—A completion date should be set.

Challenging—Your goals should be a stretch upward.

Sample SMART+C Goals for Increasing Rigor in Your School

S—Increase the overall rigor in our school by increasing the level of tasks, projects, and assignments to Level 3 of Webb's Depth of Knowledge.

M—By the end of the year, at least 60% of tasks, projects, and assignments will be at Level 3 of Webb's Depth of Knowledge.

A—Since we are already at about 20% on Level 3, over the year, teachers will work together to increase to 60%.

R—This goal is based on our mission of helping each student learn and grow to his or her highest potential.

T—Our interim timeline is to be at 40% by January 5, then to 60% by the end of the school year.

C—Although this is a challenge, it will require our teachers focusing on this goal and working on it consistently.

Step 5: Develop and Implement Strategies

Next, develop and implement specific strategies and tactics that identify advocacy opportunities. Effective strategies:

- Carry out your strategy and are appropriate for your goals.
- Fit your style (one out-of-control tactic can wreck a whole campaign).
- Are doable and cost-effective.
- Make your group feel good about themselves and about what they are doing.
- Create a written time line for implementation of the selected strategies.

Step 6: Monitor and Adjust

Finally, measure, monitor, review, and revise your plan regularly. Always look for feedback on the six steps of the plan. As you monitor and review, do not be afraid to make changes in order to improve the odds for success. Use ROI (return on investment) as a key indicator for changes.

Sample Advocacy Plan

Here's an example of an initial advocacy plan.

Step 1: Describe the Issue

I work with a veteran teaching staff that wants to improve the rigor of their instruction but continues to use teaching practices that are not aligned with the needs of their students or that were state-of-the-art decades ago but no longer get the needed results. When I talk with teachers, most of them identify a need for more professional development, including coaching to support refined instructional practices.

Step 2: Identify Current Strengths and Challenges

I will introduce the topic at the next school improvement team meeting, ask for their support, and work with a subcommittee to plan a staff meeting where we will work together to identify our strengths and challenges in this area. The key will be to be supportive and nonthreatening

(Continued)

(*Continued*)

in the presentation at the school improvement team meeting and at the staff meeting.

Step 3: Identify Expected Allies and Opponents

I know that most teachers recognize the need for refining our instructional practices. They understand the changing demography of our school and community, as well as the increased pressure for improved scores on state achievement tests. Specifically, the chair and two other members of the School Improvement Team talk regularly about the issue and support changes. There is also support from the district office for strengthening and updating instructional practices. On the other hand, three of my most veteran teachers who work with the upper grades see no need to change. They overtly resist and are opposed to using resources for additional professional development.

Step 4: Be Clear About Goals and Objectives

The goal is to secure additional resources, both time and money, for professional development and to identify someone who will serve as an instructional coach to work directly with teachers on implementing the refined instructional practices.

Step 5: Develop and Implement Strategies

Once I have support from the School Improvement Team, we need to schedule a time to meet with the staff, introduce the topic, discuss current strengths and challenges, and select a planning team. I will ask the team to submit a plan, including a proposed budget, within two months for review by the School Improvement Team. I will alert my district office supervisor of our school-level work and plan to secure her support and to assist in locating resources to implement the plan.

Step 6: Monitor and Adjust

As part of the plan, I will ask that the subcommittee identify ways to monitor the implementation and success of the plan. I will also work with the School Improvement Team, once the plan is developed, to describe ways to collect data, both quantitative and qualitative, about our success and to examine that data to identify both our successes and ways to adjust and improve implementation.

Final Thoughts

If you follow the advocacy plan method, you will have completed plans that are strategical and measurable and that will lead to success. Your plan is the blueprint for your advocacy program. Sound planning, research, creativity, and thoroughness will contribute to its success.

Final Reflection Questions

What challenge do you face in this particular area of advocacy?

What was the most important thing you learned in this chapter?

How can you apply that lesson in your own situation?

In six months, if you look back on this learning, what would you like to have accomplished?

E

Engaging Through Technology

Technology is a tool for communication; if you don't use it effectively, it sends a negative message.

—Unknown

Technology has emerged as one of the most important advocacy tools. Most schools' online presence has moved beyond the traditional website to include a Facebook page (www.facebook.com), a Twitter account (www.twitter.com), YouTube (www.youtube.com), and Flickr (www.flickr.com), as well as blogs by teachers, principals, or the superintendent, for sharing videos and photos about school events. We'll look at social media as advocacy tools in Chapter K: Keys to Social Media, but in this chapter we will talk about more traditional forms of media like your school's website and email as tools for advocacy.

Your School's Website

The first place many families turn to for information about their child's school, particularly in times of severe weather or some other emergency, is the school website. School websites frequently share calendar information, student handbooks, school news, links to important outside information, and photos and videos of school activities.

While most school websites are guided by district policy, it is common for each school to have some latitude about content included on the site. Because of its high visibility, your school's website should be attractive, informative, and user-friendly enough to encourage families to return again and again for information.

When they do so, each return is an opportunity to provide information about your school and to advocate for programs, practices, and resources.

Good websites are attentive to four key elements. First, they pay attention to appearance. They use an appropriate color scheme that doesn't detract from the content. The text is visually pleasing and uses fonts that are easy to read. Graphics and photos lend visual variety and appeal. But don't overuse them, and make sure they add meaning to your written content. Finally, keep the site simple, easy to navigate, and include sufficient white space. Overloading your site with design, animation, or other effects will detract from your content.

Keep it fresh and original—One of the most important things about a web presence is the need to keep it original and fresh. Updated content is absolutely critical. People visit sites to gather information, and the presence of fresh, original content will bring them back again and again.

Know your audience—A good website recognizes the audience that will be using it and provides content that is relevant to that audience. Choose headlines and text that aligns with your audience's needs. Keep your audience in mind, and use a human voice when writing content. A conversational tone is better received than one that uses educational jargon and a formal tone.

Make it easy to navigate—A good website has content that is easy to locate and use. Name pages and links so that people will easily understand them. Routinely check to see that links are working, and make sure that most content is no more than a single click away from the homepage. If there is a lot of content, include a search box so that visitors can easily find what they are looking for.

Clean, simple, professional design—Pay attention to the look of your site. Be sure that colors contrast well and that the font of your text makes reading easy. Remember that lots of text can make locating information difficult. Use subheadings or bullet points to improve the layout.

Expand the content through links—Include links that will take users to additional content. For example, you might link to a parent resource center or information on college admissions that makes your site the "one-stop parent resource" on school-related issues. Providing unique and interesting content is a sure way to get families and community to return to your site again and again.

Expand Content Through Links

One of the ways that websites stay fresh and help with your advocacy efforts is by linking the site to content on other websites. One of the most common ways to do that is to create a principal or school blog.

> **Blogs:** A blog is basically a website that functions as an online journal or personal diary. The power of a blog is that you can make it whatever you want it to be. Many principals maintain personal blogs and link to them from their school's website. It is a tool for sharing good news about your students and your school, for updating families and community on events, or for advocating for an issue you feel strongly about. You write the content and link to other resources. Google Blogger (www.blogger.com) is a free blog with easy-to-use templates.

What Makes a Good Blog

Because blogs are so idiosyncratic and serve many different purposes, it is difficult to describe a good blog. Basically, a blog is "good" if it attracts viewers and they choose to return. But generally three criteria define the functioning of an effective blog:

1. **Frequency**—The most effective blogs include frequent postings that are compelling enough to attract readers to return to see what you are thinking and writing about.
2. **Brevity**—Blogs are best characterized by relatively brief postings on a topic that may include links to other resources or information.
3. **Personality**—Blogs are generally written in the first person and build a social link to readers by reflecting the writer's individual point of view. The blog is almost like a good friend, one you trust and one who may help you solve problems.

Source: Adapted from Rettberg (2008).

Email and ListServs

One of the most effective advocacy tools is to maintain a comprehensive, up-to-date list of contacts that you can use in your advocacy efforts. Most schools maintain a database of family emails and other contact information. Before you use that list for advocacy, be sure to check district policy.

Many schools routinely share information with families as well as with members of the community. In Jackson County, Michigan, an elementary principal sends out a weekly online newsletter to the faculty, families, and friends of his school. It includes timely information about school activities but also provides suggested readings and links to other resources. It's one way he maintains a "link" to families and community, and he knows he can rely on that link when he wants to advocate for his school.

When you use email or a ListServ to share information, be sure to do three things. First, be sure the headline for the email provides enough information to grab the reader's attention. Second, make sure the information is on topic and doesn't ramble away from the topic in the headline. The key purpose of such mailings is to share information with people of a common interest. Finally, know your audience and tailor the message for that audience. Failing to attend to these things can lead people to unsubscribe or fail to open the message.

Final Thoughts

Effective communication is a key to successful advocacy. School leaders have a variety of technology tools readily available that can be used to share information and to build support for their initiatives. This chapter discussed more traditional tools like your school's website. Social media tools will be introduced in Chapter K: Keys to Social Media.

Final Reflection Questions

What challenge do you face in this particular area of advocacy?

What was the most important thing you learned in this chapter?

How can you apply that lesson in your own situation?

In six months, if you look back on this learning, what would you like to have accomplished?

F

Framing Your Message

Concentrate all your thoughts upon the work at hand. The sun's rays do not burn until brought to a focus.

—Alexander Graham Bell

The cornerstone of your advocacy and advocacy efforts is your ability to share your knowledge about issues. This knowledge is embedded in your advocacy plan (Chapter D: Designing an Advocacy Plan). The decision makers you encounter may want only basic information in your first encounter. Remember that you have only one time to make a first impression, so it should be as strong and as positive as possible. Clarity and focus will aid your presentation. Four tools that you should have in your advocacy toolbox are (1) the Inverted Pyramid, (2) the Hook, Line, and Sinker, (3) the One-Page Fact Sheet, and (4) an Elevator Talk.

The Inverted Pyramid

One efficient way to deliver your message is to use the Inverted Pyramid approach (see next page). Developed by the news media and often taught to journalism students, the approach involves the order in which you frame the issue. The most relevant points are at the top, other details are in the middle, and general information is at the bottom of the triangle.

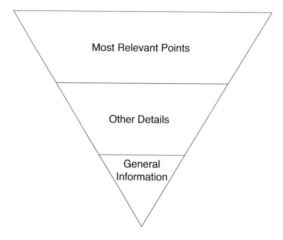

Start by describing your key information, which should include the Five Ws: who, what, when, where, and why. When you front-load your message with these key points, your audience can quickly assess whether they want to keep reading or listening to your message, but even if they stop at any later point, they will still have learned your key points. A perceived disadvantage to the inverted pyramid is that instead of building to a conclusion or satisfying ending, as with most stories, the conclusion comes first.

Hook, Line, and Sinker

A different approach used by the American Heart Association in their advocacy training is called the Hook, Line, and Sinker. The Hook is the introduction, and it paves the way for your key talking points. The Line consists of local stories, talking points, or issues, and the Sinker is the action you are requesting. This outline gives you a knowledge base to be effective with all groups or individuals you may be working with.

Either of the preceding approaches can be applied in the following two tools: the One-Page Fact Sheet and the Elevator Talk.

The One-Page Fact Sheet

A One-Page Fact Sheet helps you organize the important facts and points of your issue. It can be used as a handout to be shared with others, and it will give the necessary background information, as well as giving you added confidence when discussing your issue. One page is your limit. Most decision makers want the basic facts and don't want to waste time. Keeping to this limit also helps keep your message focused.

Key Points in a One-Page Fact Sheet

- Clearly define the issue.
- State your position on the issue.
- Clarify what you want the decision maker to do. Define five talking points in order of importance. Provide two references to support your view.
- Make the sale with a closure statement.

Mike Matkovich, a teacher-leader, used this process to develop a One-Page Fact Sheet related to increasing rigor at his high school. With his permission, we adapted it slightly for illustrative purposes.

Sample-One Page Fact Sheet:
Increasing Rigor at XXX High School

Our Goal—To provide students with high-quality and high-intensity classes in high school for postsecondary success.

Recommendation—Implement a thorough review of all courses and support appropriate revisions to ensure that each of our students is prepared for postsecondary success.

Important Facts

- Most Americans do not believe that schools provide a rigorous enough high school experience.
- The fastest growing part of the high school curriculum at the moment is AP classes or college-level courses. The fastest growing part of the college curriculum is remedial or high school classes.
- Student readiness for college-level reading is at its lowest point in more than a decade. Additionally, high school tests address content that does not exceed the ninth- or tenth-grade level.
- The most common misconception about college readiness is that meeting their high school graduation requirements prepares them for college. High schools in states with more demanding graduation standards make more progress in advancing student achievement than schools in states with less rigorous standards.

(Continued)

(*Continued*)

- Improving college readiness is crucial to the development of a diverse and talented labor force that is able to maintain and increase U.S. economic competitiveness throughout the world.

Our Situation

Fewer than 30% of our students take advanced courses. Even though 95% of our students pass the exit exam, they are not necessarily prepared for college. Fifteen percent of our students lose their scholarships at the end of their freshman year, due to a low GPA. A recent outside evaluation recommended that we increase rigor in all classes.

References

ACT. "Solutions for K–12 Education, College, and Career Readiness. The ACT Test." www.act.org

Southern Regional Education Board. "Where Policy Meets Practice." www.sreb.org

Elevator Talk

Sometimes, you have only a brief opportunity to make personal contact with a key decision maker. And the old adage is right: You have only one chance to make a first impression. In those cases, you should be prepared to give a personal story about the importance of your issue. Elevator talks, named after the time it takes an elevator to travel one or two floors, should be short and no more than 30 seconds. People tire quickly of tedious talk about an issue, particularly in a casual encounter.

Elements of an Elevator Talk

- Your name and what you do
- Your issue
- What you would like the person to know

An elevator talk may feel awkward or even feel phony at first. But treat it as an opportunity to share a story or a bit of information about you and your issue. Practice with another person by telling your story and why you care about the issue. This will give you confidence when you have a chance or planned meeting with a stakeholder or "mover and shaker." Having an effective Elevator Talk is an important advocacy tool in networking, engaging partners, and making new connections. First impressions are easily sabotaged with an Elevator Talk that's unimpressive because it's too long or too short.

Imagine you want to explain to fifth-graders the importance of greater rigor in classrooms. You use no jargon or fuzzy words, just simple talk. Now increase the grade level while maintaining the simplicity. Use 20 words or less. Refine and edit your presentation until you have a creative way of conveying your message that stimulates the listener to support your effort. Finally, write your polished message.

Final Thoughts

Learning how to frame your message is one of the most important skills you need to develop. If you don't take the time to plan your message, when you have opportunities to communicate with stakeholders, it's likely that your message won't be as effective.

Final Reflection Questions

What challenge do you face in this particular area of advocacy?

What was the most important thing you learned in this chapter?

How can you apply that lesson in your own situation?

In six months, if you look back on this learning, what would you like to have accomplished?

G

Gaining Support with Limited Resources

In a time of tight budgets, difficult choices have to be made. We must make sure our very limited resources are spent on priorities. I believe we should have no higher priority than investing in our children's classrooms and in their future.

—Bob Riley

Virtually every school or district, as well as many nonprofits, struggle with finding the resources for advocacy. In some states, schools are explicitly prohibited from using public funds to try to shape or influence public opinion. Limited resources can be a real problem when advocating for a change in your school's program.

As schools have wrestled with the issue of limited funding, certain strategies have been identified for dealing with this dilemma. Each of the strategies requires a commitment to a more collaborative and inclusive environment, one where different opinions and points of view are welcome.

The strategies fall into three broad categories: (1) business and community partnerships, (2) grants and entrepreneurial activity, and (3) use of traditional and social media.

Business and Community Partnerships

Business Partnerships

Business partnerships are most often established between a school or district and a local business partner or national partner with a local presence. The Council for Corporate and School Partnerships, founded by Coca-Cola, defines partnerships as "a mutually supportive relationship between a business and a school . . . in which the partners commit themselves to specific goals and activities intended to benefit the students and the school." Business partners often recognize that they can benefit from being seen as a supporter of schools in their community.

In DuPage, Illinois, the high school's Business-Education Partnership Council is organized and staffed by the district's information and public affairs office. Members of the council meet monthly to explore how members of the local business community can support the school, advocate for resources, and work with its members to support the school's focus on student achievement and increased community outreach and involvement.

Similarly, in Cecil County, Maryland, the Business and Education Partnership Advisory Council, a group organized by local businesses, seeks to find ways that local businesses can support the schools and advocate for students to meet job market needs and to have satisfying careers that will make them good citizens in their community. Not only do members of the council provide resources for the schools, they also serve as advocates to the larger community about specific school needs or programs.

Community Partnerships

Community partnerships bring together the resources of local businesses, service clubs, nonprofit agencies, volunteers, churches, colleges and universities—almost anyone with an interest in children and young people. They are a powerful social resource that schools can tap into to support their educational programs.

In many communities, local fraternal organizations are looking for ways to support local programs. Often they want speakers for their meetings and luncheons. It's an easy way to build relationships with a vital community group and at the same time advocate for your school, its programs, and initiatives.

Strategies for Success with Partnerships

When you work with business or community partners, follow this advice:

- **Provide high-quality information**—Help people understand the issues, as well as the school's programs and areas of need. If advocating for a new program, provide factual information with ample data about the impact on students and the way local businesses can be supportive.
- **Have a consistent message**—People rely on those they trust (including social media friends) for information. Those they trust may not necessarily be school leaders. So invest in "internal public relations" to make sure everyone in the school, as well as those working with partners, provides the same message about programs, their impact, and their value.
- **Maintain confidentiality**—Be careful what you say and to whom you say it. When working with partners, always clarify what can be shared and with whom.
- **Address key issues directly**—Deal with real concerns as soon as possible. Gather additional information that might be requested. Don't dodge issues and concerns. Make sure messages are accurate and lessen rumors.
- **Don't make promises**—Statements made early can feel like a commitment, and trust will be damaged if your "promise" can't be kept.
- **Value dissent**—Recognize that different points of view are always uncomfortable but important. They often reveal problems that weren't thought about, and they can give you clues about resistance you may encounter.

Grants and Entrepreneurial Activity

You can become much more aggressive in seeking grants and engaging in entrepreneurial activity to support your advocacy efforts. When faced with a lack of district resources to expand their curriculum, a consortium of five small Oregon districts sought a state grant to pay for adding interactive television so that they could share teachers of Spanish, accelerated math, and chemistry. Teachers rotated among the five high schools but were able to interact with students on all campuses. This same consortium shared the costs of a grant writer and, by the end of the first year, found that the new grants justified the grant writing expense.

Some schools also use entrepreneurial activity to raise funds to support program enhancements. In some cases, they create products for sale outside of school, but most of the time they involve retail operations housed within a school, often food and beverage sales.

Some high schools we've worked with have school stores that sell supplies and spirit wear. Others have a coffee shop open before and after school. Still others have a smoothie shop. In several cases, local foundations provided the seed money, including equipment and initial inventory to start the business, and local citizens contributed their services to help with financial management. In each case, students learned about managing a business and raising revenue, and the school was able to build valuable partnerships with business and community groups, a form of advocacy.

Traditional and Social Media

Both Chapter E: Engaging Through Technology and Chapter K: Keys to Social Media discuss the use of various forms of media as advocacy tools. We won't repeat that information here, but it is important to recognize the powerful way that both traditional media like websites and email, as well as social media like Facebook, Twitter, and Instagram, can be used to share information about your school and your programs and initiatives.

It's critical to balance the two approaches. Often traditional media like email or the school's website is viewed as providing a limited, somewhat biased view of the school. In other words, it's seen as an administrative tool. Social media, on the other hand, is often viewed more positively and is seen as more responsive, more up-to-date, and more engaging.

Similarly, social media is more likely accessed by younger families and newer members of your school community. Your school's website and email may not be the first source of information for many families.

Regardless, each of these forms of media, once in place, is a low-cost way to share information about your school, its students, and their successes.

Final Thoughts

Advocating for your school and its programs doesn't require a lot of resources. When resources are limited, there are several low-cost ways to share the news about your school and your efforts to improve student learning.

As discussed in other chapters, building relationships with key stakeholders and sharing your message broadly are keys to successful advocacy.

Final Reflection Questions

What challenge do you face in this particular area of advocacy?

What was the most important thing you learned in this chapter?

How can you apply that lesson in your own situation?

In six months, if you look back on this learning, what would you like to have accomplished?

H

Handling the Media

The traditional media is still important; they have just moved to new systems of delivery.

—Unknown

It's an age when people have incredible access to information. The media provides information 24/7 through television, radio, print sources, and the Internet. Whether we are attempting to provide a positive image to the public and key decision makers or dealing with a crisis, one of the most effective keys of sharing fast-breaking information with the public is to tap into this information stream. We need to know what is newsworthy about our organization's activities and work with the media to maximize coverage. In Chapter K: Keys to Social Media, we'll focus on social media. This chapter will focus on the more traditional forms of media.

The traditional media has many forms that include local and state newspapers, television, radio, and magazines. But other media opportunities move beyond the common options. It's important to consider all the media possibilities available to you.

Examples of Other Media Opportunities

- "Shopper" newspapers
- Printings of supplements on special subjects
- Ethnic group publications
- Retiree publications
- Service clubs
- Girl or Boy Scouts publications

Identifying Media Outlets

In order to successfully use the media, you must understand the types of media available to you. Your success will depend on a media list that must be continually updated. Use a planning template similar to the following one to identify the media that is pertinent to you.

Identification of Media Outlets

Type	Options	Your Notes
Television (national, state, local, and cable)	Regular news Talk shows Commentaries Features	
Radio (national, state, local, public)	Regular news Talk shows Commentaries Features	
Newspapers (national, state, local, weekly, and daily)	News stories Features Opinion/editorial options Letters to the editor Guest columns Education sections	
Other print media	Specialty publications Newsletters Organizational mailings	

Changing Media Environment

In the past, the media operated with fixed datelines and a fixed publication schedule. While that is true for some media outlets, almost all newspapers, as well as television and radio outlets, have an online presence. Online sites are continuously updated with news stories and information. In fact, for most major publications, stories are published online before they ever appear in print.

Throughout southeastern Michigan, as well as other states, local newspapers are disappearing. Recently the entire chain of local papers in the Detroit area converted to an online format. Similarly, *The Ann Arbor News* switched from daily to twice-a-week print editions while offering a comprehensive online edition available at no cost to local readers. Perhaps more important for advocacy, readers are able to comment on stories, and those comments, right or wrong, get wide dissemination among the public.

These changes are just another manifestation of the changing media environment, at the local, state, and national levels. That means information will continue to be distributed faster and more broadly than any time in the past.

Once you identify the media source, you will need to determine the specific personnel who are important. There are four questions that, when answered, can help you identify the persons in the media with whom you plan to collaborate.

Guiding Questions

- Do you know who covers education issues?
- Do you know that person's deadlines?
- Do you know the chain of command at this media outlet?
- Do you know what the media outlet's target audience is?

Building Relationships

Developing positive strategic relationships with media personnel is the next step. Building a relationship takes time and requires persistence and effort on your part. You can take several vital actions to develop a relationship with key people. First, establish a repeatable pattern that integrates Twitter and email to engage media without annoying them. This increases your visibility and positions you as a resource and a potential source of information. Next, develop a specific process so that they will take your calls and meet with you in person. Maximize an in-person media visit or phone call. Go above and beyond the usual expectations. This will set you apart from others, who are more passive in their dealings with the media. Finally, regular contact is always a plus in relationships. In subtle ways, keep yourself in the forefront of all the people with whom they deal.

Effective Media Interviews

You can improve your effectiveness when being interviewed in the media in many ways. You want to be sure your message comes across (see Chapter F: Framing Your Message). However, people in the media also have an agenda. For them, reporting includes the basics: who, what, when, where, why, and how. Anticipating these questions will help prepare you for interviews. Additionally, keep in mind the following tips.

Tips for Talking with the Media

- Preparation is your best friend. Learn as much as you can about the reporter, the show, and the audience.
- Establish your communication goals for each interview.
- Determine two or three key points to make in order to reach your goal.
- Speak in "memorable language."
- Learn and use the "bridging technique." Redirect the interview to your key points.
- Practice, practice, practice. Practice on camera if possible.
- Do not wear clothes or use mannerisms that distract from your message.
- Forget jargon, now and forever.
- Make sure that the mind is in gear before the mouth travels.
- Look at the reporter when answering questions; turn to the camera when delivering a key point.
- Steady eyes suggest honesty; blinking, darting eyes suggest nervousness and dishonesty.
- Anticipate questions and have answers ready. Once the interview is scheduled, try to figure out what questions the reporter might ask.
- Relax.

Brad Phillips, in *The Media Training Bible* (2013), gives other additional hints for successful interviews:

- Understand the ground rules for working with reporters.
- Create memorable media messages.
- Deliver a winning interview and answer tough questions.
- Adjust your approach for print, radio, TV, and social media.
- Use positive body language that reinforces your message.
- Prepare for and manage a media crisis.

Develop a Media Team

The last step in the media process is the selection of a media team or subcommittee. Due to the range of traditional media, as well as social media opportunities, it is unrealistic to ask one person to fulfill all the responsibilities. When Barbara was teaching, the local newspaper ran a monthly page of education news. Schools were encouraged to provide information. As the newspaper faculty sponsor, Barbara assigned one student to write the monthly column. Although she and the principal provided guidance and reviewed the column, the student generally handled it. Consider your personnel resources and build on their strengths to develop your group. Finally, be sure that each member of your team understands his or her role, the guidelines, and any limitations.

The Media in a Crisis Situation

It's particularly important that you have a plan for communicating with families and the media in crisis situations. Have a system for providing families with accurate, up-to-date information about the event. For example, all information to the media should come from authorized personnel who are identified in advance. Remember that media representatives can be persistent in gaining interviews. Although you can't control what people say, especially on social media, it is important to work with your teachers and other stakeholders on how to respond to media requests. Understand that comments to the media—again, especially social media—can go viral very quickly. Someone must monitor social media to see what people are saying, so that you can respond. Inaccurate messages take on a life of their own, especially when shared again and again. We'll look at social media as a way to respond in a crisis in Chapter K: Keys to Social Media.

Final Thoughts

Traditional media is still a powerful advocacy tool. Identify key media outlets, prepare for effective interviews, enhance your writing skills, develop your team, and utilize the media to get your message across.

Final Reflection Questions

What challenge do you face in this particular area of advocacy?

What was the most important thing you learned in this chapter?

How can you apply that lesson in your own situation?

In six months, if you look back on this learning, what would you like to have accomplished?

I

Internal and External Stakeholders

Find the appropriate balance of competing claims by various groups of stakeholders. All claims deserve consideration but some claims are more important than others.

—Warren Bennis

A stakeholder is anyone who cares about your school, district, or education in general. The stakeholder may agree or disagree with what you are doing but is concerned about what is happening. There are direct or internal stakeholders, who have a visible role in your school or district, and indirect or external stakeholders, who have an interest in your school or district but who are not directly connected to the school. Indirect stakeholders are concerned because their interests and activities may be affected, either positively or negatively, by the educational program.

Direct, or Internal, Stakeholders	Indirect, or External, Stakeholders
Teachers Principals and assistant principals Staff members, such as administrative assistants	Local businesses Community college Local colleges
District office leadership and staff school board Parents	Retirees Professional associations

It's important to consider whether individuals have a direct or indirect role because that will impact how you approach advocating with them. For example, you'll want to begin with your direct stakeholders because they are the people who are most impacted by changes. Then you'll want to advocate with indirect stakeholders, so that you can gain their support.

Ways to Advocate with Internal and External Stakeholders

Although some advocacy strategies are the same with internal and external stakeholders, you can take some specific actions with each group.

Strategies for Advocating to All Stakeholders

- Personal conversations
- One-page fact sheets
- Newsletters/emails
- Social media postings
- Sharing success stories

Strategies for Advocating to Direct/Internal Stakeholders	Strategies for Advocating to Indirect/External Stakeholders
Sharing information during faculty meetings Highlighting classroom and student successes Asking teacher-leaders to share how the change would positively impact students	Presenting information sessions to community groups, such as the Rotary Club or Chamber of Commerce Holding community meetings Visiting local churches Talking with local elected officials

Here's an example of working with indirect/external stakeholders. When Barbara taught at a university, local schools had a variety of external stakeholders. First, there were local businesses interested in hiring graduates. Next, the community college was required to offer remedial introductory classes because of what they saw as unprepared students exiting high school. Finally, Barbara's university was a major supporter of the local school districts, in terms of funding, faculty support, and the provision of student teachers in the schools.

While the schools considered the university as an external/indirect stakeholder, there were also stakeholders within the university, some more involved in the schools than others. First, the dean of the College of Education and the School Partnerships director coordinated with the schools on the college's involvement, and they provided limited funding for school-based projects. Next, some schools worked with a faculty liaison, who delivered on-site support at least one day per week. Additionally, other faculty members offered professional development services as needed, and they supervised student teachers. Finally, there was a coordinator of student teachers, who placed the student teachers in schools.

Notice how much support was available to schools. However, the support was limited, so schools had to advocate in order to receive the material and nonmaterial resources they needed. That is the importance of identifying and advocating to your indirect/external stakeholders. They can have a positive impact on your school or district's success.

Movers and Shakers

Whether a group is a direct or indirect stakeholder, every community has a set of movers and shakers. They are recognized leaders in their area, ones to whom others turn for guidance on important issues. Each of them is someone who is able to get things done by rallying support, identifying resources, and building coalitions.

Characteristics of Movers and Shakers

- Articulate spokespersons
- Respected for their knowledge
- Able to convince others of their point of view
- Skilled at identifying and securing resources
- Connected to other movers and shakers
- Wield power and influence
- Often energetic initiators of change
- Seen as able to influence the future

Think about your direct and indirect stakeholders. Make a list of the groups and then focus on them. If you list parents, you need to identify specific parents who lead others. This may be your PTA/PTO president, but it may be another parent who is particularly vocal. There might also be a mover and shaker who does not have children in your school but who is vocal with parents. Also describe why you included each person on your list.

Next, who are the movers and shakers in your district? What characteristics do they possess? Finally, consider people outside your immediate area. Frequently, the most influential movers and shakers are outside your school or district. They may be influential politicians, policy makers, or community development personnel.

One concern we hear is that there are movers and shakers who aren't supporters of the school. Do you still need to consider them? Our response? Yes! Movers and shakers are influential and have the ability to convince others of their points of view. Since they are respected for their knowledge on a topic, it is important to develop a plan for sharing information with them that might change their opinion.

We worked in one district that actively sought "known dissenters" and invited them to be involved in improvement projects. After all, you'll hear from them sooner than later. So the district brought them into the process early. Imagine the impact when a known dissenter is part of a group supporting one of your initiatives. There's no assurance that providing information or involving them in improvement projects will change their minds. But it certainly can't hurt.

Final Thoughts

As you plan your advocacy efforts, it's important to consider all your stakeholders, whether they are directly or indirectly involved in your school. Both types of stakeholders impact what you are doing and can either support or argue against your efforts. Within those groups, there are movers and shakers, leaders who make a difference with other stakeholders. Identifying these persons and focusing your advocacy efforts on them will be part of your success as an advocate.

Final Reflection Questions

What challenge do you face in this particular area of advocacy?

What was the most important thing you learned in this chapter?

How can you apply that lesson in your own situation?

In six months, if you look back on this learning, what would you like to have accomplished?

J

Juggling Information

We have largely traded wisdom for information, depth for breadth. We want to microwave maturity.

—John Ortberg Jr.

> A special thank-you to Dr. Frank Buck, author of *Get Organized! Time Management for School Leaders*, for writing this chapter.

Today's world is information rich. In order to be an effective advocate, we must be able to research information that supports our cause.

Its abundance can be a doubled-edged sword. On the one hand, we are but a Google search away from detailed information about our passion. On the other hand, keeping up with the wealth of information presents its own set of challenges. Regardless of the amount of information available to us, it is useless unless we can find what we need when we need it.

In this chapter, we will explore the usual sources of information and how to store it so that we can retrieve it.

Email

Email is the most efficient method of written communication we have. Unfortunately, a large percentage of professionals do not use it well. In-boxes containing thousands of messages are not uncommon. Some of those messages call for us to do something. Others are reminders of meetings to attend with stakeholders or legislators. Other still contain information to save for documentation purposes.

The problem lies in that all of those messages are mixed together. Making email work involves deciding what a message means to you, as an advocate, and moving it to the right place.

In Chapter T: Time, Friend or Foe? our discussion centers around using a digital task list. If you use Outlook for this purpose, you can drag an email to the Task button. Outlook creates a new task. The entire body of the email appears in the note section of the task. Your job is to supply a name for that task that is descriptive of the exact action you need to take. Add a due date and save the task. You can now delete or archive the email.

Similarly, if you use a web-based task manager, it will likely include a special email address. Any email forwarded to that address will appear on your list. Again, the entire body of the email message appears in the attached note. Getting to-dos out of email and on your task list is a huge first step in clearing the clutter and helping you master the art of follow-through.

The second big problem for advocates is the amount of email correspondence they feel they need to keep in order to document both their efforts and the communications they receive. The sentiment is on point. However, the in-box is the wrong place to keep it.

In Outlook, create one folder for all email that is being saved for documentation purposes. Then drag all of those emails being saved for this reason from the in-box to that created folder. If you use Gmail, the Archive button serves the same purpose. When you click on All Mail, you will be able to search for any email you had sent or archived.

Paper

The paperless office is far in the future for most of us. As you advocate for your cause, you will receive letters. You will accumulate documents. You will produce material that tells your story. Having a logical system will save your desk from becoming your filing cabinet.

In *Get Organized! Time Management for School Leaders*, Frank Buck talks about classifying all files into three categories:

1. **Reference**—These folders would likely be found in filing cabinets in the corner of the office or in an adjoining file room. No action is needed on them. You simply need to be able to access the information when and if you need it.

2. **Current projects**—Keep these in a desk or credenza drawer close at hand.
3. **Fingertip files**—We all have a few folders that we use every day. For the advocate, these folders might include contact information for legislators, letterhead for the organization, lists of potential donors, and the like. Keep this information in a desk drawer so that it is literally at your fingertips.

Never let a file folder serve as a reminder. Decide the to-do associated with the folder and put it on your task list. Put the folder in your filing system. Those who are in the habit of putting sticky notes on folders quickly accumulate piles of folders.

Digital Documents

Once you have created a logical filing system for paper, create a *parallel* system for the digital documents related to your cause. On your computer desktop, create three folders:

1. **Documents**—This folder will be the parallel of the metal filing cabinet. The names of the folders within it will parallel the names of the folders in the cabinet.
2. **Current projects**—Opening this folder will provide a snapshot of your unfinished work. Are you in the process of writing a letter to your local legislator but need additional information before you complete it? Put it in your Current Projects folder on your computer's desktop. When you complete the letter, you can move it to the appropriate folder in the Documents library.
3. **Fingertip**—Your organization's letterhead in digital form will likely live here. Telephone lists you receive digitally might live here as well. If you are accessing a digital document daily, having it in your Fingertip file saves time over retrieving it from several layers deep in your filing system.

When your digital files parallel your paper ones, filing and finding information become quicker.

Digital Notes

As an advocate, you will find yourself in town hall meetings and other public events. You will be taking notes, photographs, and even audio notes. However, the notes are stored with other notes in one app, the photos are stored with other photos somewhere else, and the audio is stored with other audio files. How can you put all of the information from a meeting in one place?

Software such as Evernote or OneNote allows you to store all that information together in a single note. You will organize the information into so-called notebooks. The names of those notebooks should parallel the naming configurations you used in your paper and digital document systems.

Online Information

As you advocate for your cause, you will find information online that will support your beliefs. Other information will be in opposition to your efforts, and you need to be aware of what the other side is saying. You need a way to organize all of this information. You can use either of two easy methods for handling this job.

1. **Google Bookmarks**—Go to Google.com/bookmarks. If you are logged into your Google account, you will have access to those bookmarks from anywhere. Begin by dragging the bookmarklet to the browser's Bookmarks bar. Each time you run across a site you wish to add to your system, click that bookmarklet. A box opens. The page title and URL will already be completed. Add a "tag." The tags you use should parallel the names you used for your paper, digital documents, and digital notes. When you visit your Google Bookmarks to retrieve information, clicking on a tag returns all of the related resources.
2. **Dragging URLs**—Just to the left of any URL in the address is some type of icon. You have probably created shortcuts in the past by dragging one of those icons to the desktop. You can also create a shortcut by dragging the icon into any folder on your computer.

Social Media

In the next chapter (Chapter K: Keys to Social Media), we'll look more deeply at social media and its role in your advocacy efforts. But telling your story has never been easier. Many find social media overwhelming much like other sources of information. Use Hootsuite (Hootsuite.com) to organize your various social media outlets.

You might configure the streams within Hootsuite as follows:

- **Mentions**—Every time someone mentions your organization's Twitter name, you will see it here.
- **Retweets**—Each time someone retweets a message you have composed on Twitter, you will know it.

- **Search streams**—Does your cause have a hashtag related to it? Create a search stream. When people use that hashtag in their tweets, you will see it.
- **Scheduled messages**—One of the beauties of Hootsuite is that you can compose information now and schedule it to post on a date and time of your choosing. You can also compose the same message and send it through several different social media platforms.
- **Lists**—You will likely follow many people or organizations on Twitter. The information for some will be more important to you than the information from others. You might have a list called Legislators. Follow members of your legislative delegation and assign them to that list. In Hootsuite, you can create a stream that will display the tweets from these particular people.

Uniting the Heart and the Mind

As an advocate, your aim is for decision makers and the public at large to share your beliefs. Information is the vehicle through which you make that happen. If you can assemble and organize good information, be able to find it when you need it, and deliver it with passion to reach both the hearts and the minds of others, your mission will have been a success.

Final Thoughts

Today we have access to so much information—some reliable, some less so. It's easy to get overwhelmed with all we read online or the emails we receive. Successful advocates develop a system to organize that information so that it can be successfully accessed and deployed to share their issue.

Final Reflection Questions

What challenge do you face in this particular area of advocacy?

What was the most important thing you learned in this chapter?

How can you apply that lesson in your own situation?

In six months, if you look back on this learning, what would you like to have accomplished?

K

Keys to Social Media

Smart phones and social media expand our universe. We can connect with others or collect information easier and faster than ever.

—Daniel Goleman

Social media has become one of the nation's most important tools for communication, and most school leaders recognize the power of social media to shape and mold public opinion. It is that power that makes social media an effective advocacy tool.

A recent study found that most principals believe that social networking can positively impact their communication. More than half of principals belong to at least one social networking site. Principals are also frequent users of webinars, YouTube, and podcasts as part of their professional lives.

While it is easy to dismiss social networking as a fascination of teenagers and college students, to do so minimizes one of the fastest growing trends in technology, the ability to easily and quickly connect with others and with information about groups and organizations.

Various forms of social media have quickly spread beyond the young and are now used by businesses and professionals around the world to find jobs, to market products and services, and to connect with new clients.

Why You Should Pay Attention to Social Media

- **It builds relationships**—Creating relationships is important for leaders, and social media is a new and very effective way to build support among your stakeholders.
- **It's about customers**—Parents and employees often come from a different generation, one that wants to work differently and to be involved in the educational process. Social media is a way to engage them in the life of your school.
- **They're already talking**—Check out the Internet and other online sites. People are already commenting about your school and about your leadership.
- **Listen as well as share**—The principal is responsible for maintaining the school's image. Use social media to interact with parents and community. Use it both to hear from them and to share information. It can provide a way to detect rumors and allow you to respond quickly.
- **You'll be well received**—Almost everyone we've talked with reports the positive reception they got to having a blog, a Twitter feed, or a school Facebook page.
- **It builds community**—People commit to things they care about. As previously described, the public is less trustful of schools. Social media promotes community by inviting people to be part of the conversation.
- **It's here to stay**—Even as the forms of social media continue to change, the evidence is that our use of the tools will only accelerate. Increasingly, the expectation is that schools stay connected to their families and their community. Social media is the tool.

Source: Adapted from Porterfield & Carnes (2010).

The online presence of many schools has evolved beyond the school website and often includes several social media sites. A school Facebook page (www.facebook.com), along with Twitter (www.twitter.com), YouTube (www.youtube.com), and Flickr (www.flickr.com) accounts, is common. One of the advantages of these sites is that they are free. But one of the challenges is the need to maintain and update your presence on these sites.

Rules for Communication Using Social Media

- Stick to your area of expertise and provide unique, individual perspectives on your school.
- Post only useful and respectful comments.
- Always pause and think before you post anything.
- If you disagree with others' comments, keep it polite and appropriate.
- Respect confidentiality.

Source: Intel Corporation, 2010.

Facebook

Facebook has become a worldwide phenomenon. Founded in 2004, Facebook has grown exponentially until today more than half of Americans have a Facebook account. Facebook has also become the most frequently used social media site for youth and adults. A presence on Facebook helps to build your school's image as one that is comfortable and that has a more transparent communication presence.

Why a Facebook Presence?

Social media can help create a community where your students, teachers, families, and community can gather and share information, interact, and build your school's image and reputation. That's a powerful tool for your advocacy efforts.

Increasingly, families and community turn to online resources as a way to learn about schools and other educational organizations, to identify their strengths and challenges, and to assist in making decisions about school programs and placement.

Having a presence on Facebook helps to establish your school as one that is comfortable with a more transparent presence and allows you to more quickly disseminate information about your school. Always build a link to your school's Facebook account from the school website.

Twitter

Another powerful social media tool is Twitter. Each entry is limited to no more than 140 characters and is based on a simple concept: People want to know what others are doing. It is a way to provide short updates and deliver those updates quickly and efficiently to followers of your Twitter account.

People use Twitter to communicate, to ask directions, to seek advice, to share ideas and information, and to exchange thoughts. Schools and other businesses increasingly use Twitter to make announcements and share important news.

As with Facebook, Twitter offers the option of a corporate Twitter account, which is used commonly by schools. These accounts provide a way to enhance its online presence while having greater control over the message and the image. One of the major advantages of a corporate Twitter account is the ability to prevent unwanted tweets from being published, those that may detract from your school and your message.

With a Twitter account, your school can quickly provide followers with up-to-date information about things like school closings, student activities, awards and recognitions, and upcoming events for parents. It is a great way to share the accomplishments of your students and your teachers.

11 Ways Your School Can Use Twitter

As we've watched schools use social media, we've identified ways that you can use Twitter to promote your school:

1. Tweeting photos and brief biographies about new teachers
2. Sharing information about new programs
3. Posting your schools' sports scores and results
4. Sharing the daily lunch menu
5. Posting changes to your schedule
6. Announcing upcoming meetings and events
7. Sharing educational news and articles about your school and program
8. Tweeting a school photo of the day
9. Posting short videos about school concerts or drama performances
10. Announcing opportunities to volunteer at your school
11. Tweeting recognitions and awards for students and staff

A Twitter account is a great advocacy tool and a way to share information with families and community. Increasingly, parents and other stakeholders use their mobile phones to access their Twitter accounts and stay in touch with friends. This provides almost simultaneous access to parents and others and provides one way to nurture and sustain your school's relationship with these groups. Don't forget to establish a link between your school's website and your Twitter account.

YouTube and Flickr

In addition to a presence on Facebook and Twitter, many schools have begun to use YouTube for posting videos of school events and Flickr to post photos of school activities. Both sites are free and provide a quick and easy way to store and share information about your school.

You can also build links between both sites and other communication tools like your school's website or your Facebook and Twitter accounts.

10 Ways Your School Can Use YouTube and Flickr for School Communications

YouTube
1. Post a video of school concerts and dress rehearsals
2. Share a video of recent sports events
3. Post a video orientation to your school
4. Create a video that introduces your new teachers
5. Post a video to share information from a school assembly
6. Share a safety video for use in science labs

Flickr
7. Share photos from recent school activities
8. Create a photo library about recognitions and awards your school receives
9. Post a school photo of the day or week
10. Create a photo orientation packet to introduce your school to new students and their families

Challenges of Using Social Media for Advocacy

Establishing your initial presence on social media sites may be the easiest task. The greater challenge is to maintain, nurture, and sustain your presence. We've identified these challenges to maintaining your social media presence.

Management and monitoring required—Social media sites must remain current and up-to-date if they are to be a viable tool for communication.

That means someone has to be responsible for adding content and for policing the sites to monitor comments added by people who "friend" your site.

Current, fresh content—All forms of social media thrive on current content. You will need to update your sites routinely, preferably daily. The task is easier if you link accounts so that the content on one can be accessed on others. But the key is to monitor your audience and provide them with the information that will attract them to return.

Be careful not to offend—When posting items on any social media account, be attentive to word choices and the types of events and activities you showcase. Use inclusive language, and select a variety of things to discuss. Social media can provide instant communication but also create instant controversy.

Be careful what you post—In particular, be careful about posting videos and photos of students without obtaining permission from their parents. Many families are reluctant to have identifiable information about their children readily available on the Internet.

Final Thoughts

Social media has changed the way schools communicate with parents and their school community. But it's clear that they are seen as a vital source of information by a generation of families that is more comfortable with technology and more "plugged in" than prior generations. That's what makes social media such a valuable resource for your advocacy efforts.

Final Reflection Questions

What challenge do you face in this particular area of advocacy?

What was the most important thing you learned in this chapter?

How can you apply that lesson in your own situation?

In six months, if you look back on this learning, what would you like to have accomplished?

L

Local Advocacy Is Foundational

All politics is local.

—Tip O'Neil

"All politics is local" still rings true today. A major key to effective advocacy efforts is the developing and maintaining of strategic alliances with local residents and officials. A wide range of people help shape community policies, and the relationships you develop with them will determine the success or failure of your advocacy efforts.

This chapter will help you identify the different stakeholders in your community and how they can help you be successful in your advocacy efforts. The more people who join in your advocacy effort, the more power your group will have to influence educational change. It must be a team effort.

Three types of local groups can impact your activities. First, there are those in elected positions. Next, you have internal stakeholders who are connected with your school. Finally, there are external stakeholders. The following chart identifies the contacts that are essential for you to involve in your local efforts.

Elected*	Internal	External
Mayor County/town manager Town council County administrator School superintendent School board members	Teachers Staff Students Administrative team PTAs/PTOs	Families Community movers and shakers Nonprofits Media Business leaders Senior citizens Local college Community colleges

*Depending on your local situation, some of those listed under elected officials may be appointed.

Many of the individuals on this list will become your partners. Some may well be those to whom you are making your advocacy request. Knowing your supporters as well as those with opposing views gives you an advantage in planning. Key contacts are those with the movers and shakers in your community. Use your contacts to identify this group. See Chapter I: Internal and External Stakeholders for more information.

Elected Officials

In working with local elected officials, a major benefit is that those running for office are your neighbors. They may live down the street from you or across town but are still close enough for you to know them. Locally, there are many opportunities for you to get involved and advocate for your school. Consider offering to help your locals with research on issues if they do not have the staff to do this. Position yourself as a dependable source of pertinent and credible information on education. Remember to focus on issues as a nonpartisan participant. Finally, do not burn bridges with your local elected officials on issues—you are committed for the long haul. (They often choose to run for positions at the state level.)

Committees and local boards usually meet monthly and offer time for citizen input. An important person to know is the gatekeeper who controls access to the elected official. You can also volunteer for study groups looking at an issue. Almost all local governing bodies post information about their meeting schedule and agendas online. Use that information to sign up to speak where there is an opportunity for citizen input. Be prepared with your

One-Page Fact Sheet, and leave copies with everyone at the meeting. Local elected officials may be willing to meet with you to stay informed about the key issues. Consider local coffee shops or other meeting places where informal gatherings take place to have gab sessions about daily issues. When Ron was a principal, he quickly learned the importance of Saturday morning coffee and donuts at a local bakery. Most Saturdays the conversation was not about schools, but his attendance built relationships. That meant that when a local bond issue was on the ballot, there was the opportunity to share information and build support.

You cannot do all local advocacy by yourself. It will take a well-organized group with a well-designed plan to achieve your local advocacy goals. There are five keys for success with local officials. Each is critically important.

Five Keys for Success

1. Always maintain your credibility as a source of information on education. A relationship built on trust is essential.
2. Time is a factor in working with local officials. Honor their commitment by not being a time waster. Don't be afraid to say you don't know but be clear that you will get back to them with correct information.
3. Keep in contact by updating your local officials about the issues affecting the community they represent. Success stories are great additions.
4. Supplement your communication with written material. The One-Page Fact Sheet (see Chapter F: Framing Your Message) is very effective because most officials are likely to read materials that are brief and to the point.
5. Following up with officials with a thank-you. Local officials need to be reminded that you value their support and feedback.

Internal Groups

Just as every community has a lot of stakeholders, so do schools and school districts. They include teachers and other employees, families who send their children to your school, and the students themselves.

The dilemma is that each of these stakeholder groups has different interests, and each group may consist of subgroups that can confound your message. We've found that elementary staff and elementary families have different interests than middle or high school staff and families. While there are overlapping interests, it's important to recognize the differences. That means that, when developing your advocacy plan, you will want to consider each group and how you will engage them.

Most schools and districts have regular newsletters that are shared with school staff and with families. Too often they are used as a vehicle to share information rather than as a tool for both gathering and sharing information. Include ways that families and staff can share ideas for stories or provide input on an issue.

Make sure the information doesn't focus on a single issue like high school athletics or music programs. Talk with teachers and families to figure out what information they want, and tailor newsletters to those interests.

Finally, recognize that social media has become the major way that young families learn about their child's school. The Pew Research Center's Internet & American Life Project found that almost 75% of families use social media and that many turn first to social media for information rather than traditional sources like paper newsletters, TV and radio, or even your school's website (Lenhart, 2015).

External Groups

When advocating with community groups, regular, consistent contact is key. You want to get your message across in a variety of ways, including in personal and public communications, such as letters to the editor or on a local blog. Get to know the editor of the local paper and the person responsible for education. Many communities have cable or local TV channels and are looking for programs from schools. Service clubs are almost always looking for a speaker and a way to build relationships and share information. Involving students is another civic opportunity for the importance of advocacy. Not to be overlooked are senior citizens. Programs are always popular at senior centers, and many are vocal supporters.

Final Thoughts

Because grassroots efforts are often the most effective ones, it's important to remember to build your advocacy base locally. Local people have credibility with their community. Additionally, a key message to communicate is each person's responsibility to vote—and to get our friends and neighbors to vote. Advocates will take every opportunity with every age group to prove the point that "all politics is local."

Final Reflection Questions

What challenge do you face in this particular area of advocacy?

What was the most important thing you learned in this chapter?

How can you apply that lesson in your own situation?

In six months, if you look back on this learning, what would you like to have accomplished?

M

Motivating Those Around You

Leaders must be close enough to relate to others, but far enough ahead to motivate them.

—John C. Maxwell

As you build support among stakeholders, you will also want them to help you advocate for your issues, to build capacity for them as advocates. That means you will need to motivate them to assist you. What is the difference between a motivated and unmotivated person? Think about some of the people in your circle, whether parents, teachers, or businesspersons. How do these characteristics match up?

Characteristics

High Motivation	Low Motivation
Shows interest	Lack of interest
Always striving to do more	Does the minimum
Engaged	Disengaged
Focused	Distracted
Connected to others	Disconnected from others
Secure and confident in own abilities	Concerned about self-needs
Puts forth effort	No effort

Does that look familiar? Of course, the real issue is not figuring out whether someone is motivated or not; it's understanding and dealing with the lack of motivation.

Types of Motivation

There are two types of motivation: extrinsic and intrinsic. Extrinsic motivation includes all the outside ways we try to influence someone, such as rewards or positive notes. Intrinsic motivation comes from within. With extrinsic rewards, we can get temporary results, but for long-term impact, we need to help people activate their intrinsic motivation.

It's similar to looking at the ocean. Barbara loves watching the waves, but she's only seeing the surface. She doesn't see the perilous undercurrents. Similarly, extrinsic motivation looks good, but we don't notice the dangers. Also, the true beauty of the ocean is underneath the surface. As we go deeper, there are beautiful marine creatures, fish, and coral. Instead of short-lived waves, you see long-lasting beauty. And that is intrinsic motivation.

Intrinsic Motivation

Intrinsic motivation is that which comes from within. It is internal as opposed to external. With intrinsic motivation, people appreciate their advocacy efforts for its own sake. They enjoy the feelings of accomplishment that come with successful advocacy. There are many benefits to intrinsic motivation. Intrinsically motivated people tend to prefer challenging work, are more confident about their abilities, and believe they can truly make a difference in terms of school improvement.

The Foundational Elements of Intrinsic Motivation

Intrinsic motivation has two foundational elements: People are more motivated when they *value* what they are doing and when they *believe* they have a chance for success.

Value

Stakeholders see value in a variety of ways, but the main three are relevance, activities, and relationships.

People typically see value through the relevance of what you are asking them to do. That's why we strive to show practical applications. When you implement a new initiative and want help advocating for the initiative, those you ask want to see and understand the purpose. In fact, most people have a streaming music station playing in their heads, WII-FM—what's in it for me? That's why they ask you, "Why do we need to do this?"

Adults are juggling so many demands that they prioritize activities and their attention based on how well something meets their immediate needs. So often we forget to show people why they need to know what we are doing. Teachers are more engaged in advocacy efforts when they see a useful connection to themselves.

Next, there is value in the type of activity you are doing. Adults are generally more motivated by doing something than by simply "sitting and getting." They are also more motivated when they have ownership in the activity. Rather than simply handing people a series of steps to follow, involve them in the decision-making process.

Finally, adults find value in their relationships with you and their peers. The old adage is true: "They don't care what you know until they know how much you care." Stakeholders need to feel liked, cared for, and respected by leaders. They are also motivated by working with their peers to achieve a goal. Encouraging people to work with others to advocate for your issue will help.

Belief in Success

People are also motivated when they believe they have a chance to be successful. And that belief is built on several building blocks: level of challenge, experiences, and encouragement.

First, the degree of alignment between the difficulty of an activity and a person's skill level is a major factor in self-motivation. Imagine that you enjoy playing soccer and that you have the chance to compete in a local game. You will be playing against Lionel Messi (Argentina and Barcelona), named World Player of the Year four times in six years. How do you feel? In that situation, there's plenty of opportunity for challenge—probably too much challenge! Or perhaps you love reading novels, but the only language you can read in is Russian. How motivated will you be in a literature class? This is where training is crucial. Many people are willing to participate in your advocacy efforts; they just don't know how. You'll need to provide information and support for them.

Ways to Build Feelings of Success

- Provide time for teachers to collaborate with one another to craft advocacy strategies.
- Ask someone to share an effective practice.
- Share stories about advocacy efforts.

Another building block to feelings of success is the encouragement one receives from others. Encouragement is "the process of facilitating the development of the person's inner resources and courage towards positive movement" (Dinkmeyer & Losoncy, 1980, p. 16).

When you encourage others, you accept people as they are, so that they will accept themselves. You value and reinforce their attempts and efforts and help them realize that mistakes are learning tools. Encouragement says, "Try, and try again. You can do it. Go in your own direction, at your own pace. I believe in you."

This is particularly important as someone is beginning to help with advocacy efforts. Because it's a new game, a person may feel unsure and need your encouragement.

Samples of Encouraging Phrases

- Talk with me about the successes and the challenges of what you did.
- Every time I advocate, I reflect on it and identify ways to improve. How are you doing that?

Shared Motivation

A final concept to consider is that of sharing motivation among all stakeholders. Intrinsic motivation is fostered in an overall environment of encouragement. It's important to share among one another what is working. Celebrating success should be a critical part of your plan. Use email, newsletters, and social media to ensure that everyone involved in your advocacy efforts sees the successes. Positive experiences will encourage more positive movement.

Final Thoughts

Motivation is hardwired into each individual. However, at times, people are not motivated to try something new. By creating an environment that encourages intrinsic motivation and by ensuring value and success, we can increase others' motivation.

Final Reflection Questions

What challenge do you face in this particular area of advocacy?

What was the most important thing you learned in this chapter?

How can you apply that lesson in your own situation?

In six months, if you look back on this learning, what would you like to have accomplished?

N

Networking

Pulling a good network together takes effort, sincerity and time.

—Alan Collins

A coalition or network is a group of either organizations or people who agree to work together with the focus on a common goal. Coalitions are efficient when groups have similar goals. This networking that springs from grassroots and local members working together is one of the best approaches to becoming more powerful and able to change the course of any endeavor. TEAM: Together, everyone accomplishes more.

Benefits of Coalitions and Networks

The benefits of coalition building go beyond increased power in relation to the opposition. Coalition building may also strengthen the members internally, enabling them to be more effective in other arenas. According to Brad Spangler (2003), some other key advantages to coalition building are as follows:

- A coalition of organizations can win on more fronts than a single organization working alone and can increase the potential for success.
- A coalition can bring more expertise and resources to bear on complex issues, where the technical or personnel resources of any one organization would not be sufficient.

- A coalition can develop new leaders. As experienced group leaders step forward to lead the coalition, openings are created for new leaders in the individual groups. The new, emerging leadership strengthens the groups and the coalition.
- A coalition will increase the impact of each organization's effort. Involvement in a coalition means more people have a better understanding of your issues and more people advocating for your side.
- A coalition will increase available resources. Not only will physical and financial resources be increased, but each group will gain access to the contacts, connections, and relationships established by other groups.
- A coalition may raise its members' public profiles by broadening the range of groups involved in a conflict. The activities of a coalition are likely to receive more media attention than those of any individual organization.
- A coalition can build a lasting base for change. Once groups unite, each group's vision of change broadens, and it becomes more difficult for opposition groups to disregard the coalition's efforts as dismissible or as a special interest.
- A successful coalition is made up of people who may have never worked together before. Coming from diverse backgrounds and different viewpoints, they have to figure out how to respect one another's differences and get something big accomplished. They have to figure out how each group and its representatives can make their different but valuable contributions to the overall strategy for change. This helps avoid duplication of efforts and improves communication among key players.

Disadvantages of Working in Coalitions

There are also disadvantages to working in coalitions.

- Member groups can get distracted from other work. If that happens, efforts not related to the coalition may become less effective, and the organization may be weakened overall.
- A coalition may be only as strong as its weakest link. Each member organization will have different levels of resources and experience, as well as different internal problems. Organizations that provide a lot of resources and leadership may get frustrated with other members' shortcomings in that respect.

- To keep a coalition together, it is often necessary to cater to one side more than another, especially when negotiating tactics. If some members prefer high-profile confrontational tactics, they might dislike subdued tactics, thinking they are not sufficient to mobilize support. At the same time, the low-profile conciliatory members might be alarmed by the advocates of a more confrontational style, fearing they will escalate the conflict and make eventual victory more difficult to obtain.
- The democratic principle of one group-one vote may not always be acceptable to members with a lot of power and resources. The coalition must carefully define the relationships between powerful and less powerful groups.
- Individual organizations may not get credit for their contributions to a coalition. Members that contribute a lot may think they do not receive enough credit (Spangler, 2003).

How to Build a Network or Coalition

To be most effective, you need to build a network of people who can help with your efforts. Remember, communication is a two-way street, so this group will serve two purposes: to help you understand how stakeholders in various groups perceive a situation and to help you communicate your message.

One model is the Key Communicator Network, developed by the National School Public Relations Association. It includes a series of steps that help you identify key people to invite to participate and ideas for how you can work with them to advocate for your vision.

Building a Key Communicator Network

- Bring together a small group of trusted people who know the community. Brainstorm with those whom others listen to. While the bank president may be an opinion leader, so might the barber, cab driver, bartender, or supermarket checkout clerk.
- From all the names that have been gathered, create a workable list to invite to join your network. Make sure that all segments of the community are represented.
- Send a letter to the potential members, explaining that you want to create a new communications group for your school to help the

(Continued)

(*Continued*)

community understand the challenges, successes, and activities of your school. In the letter, invite the potential members to an initial meeting and include a response form.
- Make follow-up phone calls to those who do not return the response form, especially those who will be the most important to have on your network.
- Start the initial meeting by explaining that those in the audience have been invited because you see them as respected community members who care about the education students are being provided. Also point out that you believe schools operate best when the community understands what is taking place and becomes involved in providing the best possible learning opportunities for students. Then describe the objectives of a Key Communicator Network:
  - To provide network members with honest, objective, consistent information about the school
  - To have the network members deliver this information to others in the community when they are asked questions or in other opportunities
  - To keep their ears open for any questions or concerns community members might have about the school. Those concerns should be reported to the principal or person in charge of the network so that communication efforts can deal with those concerns. (It's always best to learn about the concerns of one or two people instead of when 20 or 30 are vocally sharing those concerns with others.)
  - Ask the invitees for a commitment to serve on the network and find out the best way to communicate with them, such as email, fax, or telephone.
  - Establish a Key Communicator Network newsletter specifically for these people. After the first year, send out a short evaluation form to see how the network is working and how it might be improved.

For more information about Key Communicator Networks, contact the National School Public Relations Association (301-519-0496) and purchase a copy of *A Guidebook for Opinion Leader/Key Communicator Programs.*

Now think about your own school community. How would you build a Key Communicator Network? Use the following "Creating Your Key Communicator Network" form to develop your plan.

Creating Your Key Communicator Network

1. Whom would you bring together to talk about building a network? Whom would you talk with about the group? How would you assure that all segments of your community are represented?	
2. How will you extend an invitation to potential members and explain the purpose of the group? How will you create a sense of urgency and importance for their participation?	
3. How do you plan to organize the initial meeting? Where will the meeting be held? How will you share your vision? How will you listen and gather feedback from members?	
4. What process will you use to both gather and share information with the network? How will you keep members engaged in the work?	

Final Thoughts

Building a coalition or a network of key stakeholders is a critical part of advocacy. No matter how productive you are, you cannot be a lone advocate for positive change. By coordinating with others, you will increase your effectiveness and make more of an impact.

Final Reflection Questions

What challenge do you face in this particular area of advocacy?

What was the most important thing you learned in this chapter?

How can you apply that lesson in your own situation?

In six months, if you look back on this learning, what would you like to have accomplished?

O

Overcoming Objections

So many objections may be made to everything, that nothing can overcome them but the necessity of doing something.

—Samuel Johnson

We can't think of any initiative that didn't provoke some opposition. It's just a natural part of change and will emerge as you advocate for your issues. This chapter will focus on this resistance and on ways you can counter the tactics most commonly used to object.

You've probably heard many of the most common objections. They often sound the same regardless of the issue.

Examples of Common Objections

- We've never done it this way before.
- Everything is working now. Why should we change?
- This sounds like it will take too much time.
- We are already doing too much. Now you want to add something else?
- This is a fad. If we wait, it will go away.

(Continued)

(Continued)

- What about this, and that, and this, and that . . . ?
- Your proposal goes too far/doesn't go far enough.
- It won't work here. We're different.
- It puts us on a slippery slope.
- We can't afford this.
- You'll never convince enough people.
- We're simply not equipped to do this.

Have you ever heard any of those? Probably so. It's easy to assume that someone is just being stubborn when they say things like this. But in most cases, that isn't true. Those who resist often have legitimate questions about an initiative and seek additional information about the plan. In fact, we think it's important to appreciate your opponents and those who resist. Often they identify things that should be addressed and questions that must be answered. Resistance may not feel good, but it is a healthy and normal part of advocacy.

Resistance can come from a number of factors, including personal and professional needs. In Chapter R: Resistance to Change, we'll explore the specific aspects of resistance. Here we will discuss how to overcome particular types of objections you may face.

Tactics of Objection

Sometimes a person goes beyond basic objections in an effort to derail your plans. Objections can manifest themselves in four ways.

Tactic	Description
1. Death by delay	Endlessly putting off or diverting discussion of your idea until all momentum is lost
2. Confusion	Presenting so much distracting information that confidence in your proposal dies
3. Fear mongering	Stirring up irrational anxieties about your idea
4. Character assassination	Undermining your reputation and credibility

Source: Kotter & Whitehead (2010).

Do you recognize any of these? If you've ever experienced any of these strategies, you know it is difficult to move past them. Often the person using these tactics influences others, and the resistance can grow into a larger problem.

For example, Barbara was asked to present at an afternoon meeting in a local elementary school. She arrived just after lunch, and the principal met her at the door. He explained that the school had teacher assistants for kindergarten through second grade. However, test scores had plummeted in grades 3–5, so the principal wanted to shift the assistants to the upper grades for half the school day. He had data to support the plan, but instead of building consensus, he asked the teachers to vote on the plan. There were more K–2 teachers than 3–5, and the K–2 teachers voted no since they did not want to lose their assistants for a portion of the day. As he noted, "Now I have to go in and tell them their vote doesn't count. We are going to do it anyway."

When he shared the decision with teachers, some of the faculty used some of the tactics listed earlier. Several shared "worst-case scenarios" of what would happen to younger children if the plan went through (fear mongering), and one teacher began to accuse the principal personally (character assassination). Even though the idea of sharing assistants across all grades had merit, it never happened because of the objections of the primary teachers.

Solutions to Objections

What is the solution? Let's look at strategies you might use to diffuse each type of objection so that you can move forward with positive change.

Death by Delay

With death by delay, a teacher, parent, or other stakeholder tries to slow down discussion and action on an issue. Hopefully, by holding up the conversation, people will lose interest and move on to something else. Sometimes, a person asks for straw polls or for a task force to study the idea further. This usually occurs after you have already gathered input through conversations, surveys, and focus and leadership groups. But by asking for additional input, they stall action. A common response is "We need to study this more" or "We have too much on our plates right now—can we look at it next year?"

In order to respond to delays, be sure to use a variety of strategies to gain input and garner support for your plans. Provide a reasonable amount of time for discussion and reflection, but set a deadline and stick to it. Also, be prepared with succinct, fact-based responses to questions and comments. Referring back to earlier discussions or surveys is helpful.

Confusion

Confusion is another tactic. In this case, a person tries to derail your ideas with questions about irrelevant facts. You also might end up in a conversation that is so convoluted you cannot sustain a meaningful dialogue about the subject. Statistics are often used to confuse the issue. Although data is important, someone who is trying to confuse the issue will focus in on an outlier or find outside data that does not support your plan.

The most appropriate response to confusion is clarity. Provide clear explanations on your strategy as well as a well-defined rationale. Keep it short and simple, and when a person continues to be confusing, return to your focus on the fact.

Fear Mongering

With fear mongering, a resistant person attempts to raise anxiety and prevent a thorough examination of a proposal. People begin to worry that implementing even a good plan can be filled with frightening results. We worked in a school that was considering implementing 1:1 technology. In the teachers' workroom, there was an animated conversation about all the dangers of the plan. "What if students break them?" "If we buy the technology, we won't have money for other supplies!" The entire conversation was fear based. In this case, the principal shared information that assuaged their fears, and the implementation was successful. Once again, sharing clear information about the realistic outcomes of your plan is critical.

Character Assassination

A final type of objection is quite negative. If other tactics don't work, then opponents may turn to character assassination. They may question your competence, character, or motives. Common comments include, "She's a first year principal; she doesn't really understand." "I heard about him from his previous school. He's always trying to control things." "She's just doing this to impress the district."

This type of objection is particularly challenging, especially because it is so personal. There is no focus on the issue—only on you (or other decision makers). There are two main strategies when you face this:

1. Stay above the personal negativity. Do not respond in kind.
2. Focus on the facts, and involve other stakeholders to help balance the negativity.

Overall Strategies

Kotter and Whitehead, in their book *Buy-In* (2010), outline strategies to successfully promote and defend your idea or position, no matter the type of objection. We've adapted them for our purposes.

- Build respect from other stakeholders by allowing someone to object, even if the objection is negative. Use meeting norms and procedures to limit the time for negativity and to move the meeting in more positive directions.
- Gain support from your stakeholders with simple, clear, and commonsense responses.
- Win their hearts by, most of all, showing respect for all perspectives. Don't take objections personally.
- Constantly monitor the people whose hearts and minds you need. Focus on the broad audience, not on the few attackers.

Final Thoughts

As you are advocating for an issue or plan, recognize that there will always be objections to your ideas. Don't take things personally. Move beyond surface objections and recognize the real issues. Then, as an advocate, you can refocus the conversation on the benefits of change and garner support.

Final Reflection Questions

What challenge do you face in this particular area of advocacy?

What was the most important thing you learned in this chapter?

How can you apply that lesson in your own situation?

In six months, if you look back on this learning, what would you like to have accomplished?

P

Public Relations 101

If I was down to my last dollar, I'd spend it on public relations.

—Bill Gates

Public relations, as part of the big picture, is concerned with delivering your messages in a positive manner. Advocacy and public relations go hand in hand. Public relations is your way to communicate to the public. Its purpose is to shape decision makers' attitudes regarding your organization or project. Public relations campaigns focus on primary and secondary audiences. Additionally, a strong public relation program must have a plan to be effective.

Effective Programs

Successful public relations programs have much in common. The American Heart Association (American Heart Association, 2008) suggests the following components of an effective program when requesting support.

Six Components of an Effective PR Program

1. Know what is relevant about your local program.
2. Know the local statistics that are essential for competent decision making.
3. Know the impact of decisions.
4. Know the financial implications of your request.
5. Know how to clarify and simplify your request.
6. Know the value of local and personal stories.

How does this apply to you? Schools often look for support for new programs and initiatives. Most often, they want funding that can support planning and the acquisition of the required supplies and materials. But that support can also come in the form of partners to share information or volunteers who will help to staff a classroom or center. You may be seeking partners to be part of your network of support

Every year, we work in hundreds of elementary and secondary schools, and we see dozens of examples where schools seek either external funding for a program or support from families and community for launching a new program. In both cases, there is a need to have accurate and timely information about your plans, along with clear evidence for how you might use any additional financial resources.

You will remember we discussed a form of SMART goals in Chapter D. Let's revisit it in this context. Haughey (2014) offers a brief history of SMART.

SMART Goals

Specific
Measurable
Achievable
Realistic
Timely

For example, you may have a goal of helping the school board see the positive things that are happening in your school. That's very general and doesn't provide a specific plan for achieving your goal. Instead, adopt a more focused goal, such as improving communication with your local board of education on the subject of student involvement in extracurricular programs that complement the academic program. You can track this with SMART goals. After doing your research, you can talk with your superintendent or other supervisor about scheduling a report to the board of education on your progress. This allows you to show the board realistic and timely progress on a specific goal.

Sample SMART Goals for Public Relations

- At the end of every semester, we will share examples of student work from the new STEM program with families and community.
- Each year, we will use our school Facebook, Twitter, and Instagram accounts to recognize students honored at our end-of-the-year awards assembly.
- By the end of November, we will finalize a plan to share timely tips with families for creating a quiet place for completing homework.

Audiences

Your public relations campaigns will focus on approaches to different audiences. It means building support for your program and increasing your chances of support. Valuable media markets include newspapers and their online websites, daily and weekly newsletters, commercial and educational television and radio, public affairs programs, and social media (see Chapter K: Keys to Social Media).

Other organizations, such as county commissioners, churches, service clubs, PTAs, have newsletters or speaking options by which to make an impact. Always remember that you are a resource for the media. By customizing your approach to the different groups, you will have the most impact. PR is knowing your audience, knowing your message and then communicating it in a positive manner (see Chapter F: Framing Your Message).

Developing a Media Plan

The final step in developing your PR campaign is the development of a media plan. This media plan must clearly define your short-term and long-term PR goals and objectives because doing so serves as your roadmap. The media plan is a part of the advocacy plan, which can be found in Chapter D: Designing an Advocacy Plan.

Steps for Developing a Media Plan

- Define your short-term and long-term goals and objectives.
- Identify key media sources and contacts.
- Determine their goals, as well as how your objectives align with them.
- Create a list of specific activities and a timeline.
- Enlist people to support your efforts.
- Implement your plan.
- Assess your activities and make needed adjustments.

Consider the following questions as you develop your plan.

Questions for a Successful Public Relations Program	
What are our strengths?	
Who are our target audiences?	
What media sources should we utilize?	
How do our goals match theirs?	
What will we do?	
Who will handle each part?	
When we will do it?	
How we will assess our efforts?	
What will we do to improve?	

As you develop and implement your plan, keep in mind some general guidelines.

General Tips in Implementing a Plan

- Understand the importance of measurable objectives.
- Keep in mind your ROI (return on investment), which is essential in terms of your time commitment.
- Always learn from the results of your work.
- Build good PR leverage relationships with the movers and shakers in the community (see Chapter M: Motivating Those Around You).
- Build a list of validators, that is, strong advocates for your program.

Sample Public Relations Activities

Schools are engaged in public relations all day, every day, all year long. That includes the way students and their families are greeted at the beginning of the day to the variety of communications you use to share information with teachers, families, and community. Even the way you respond when there is a health issue among students or a disciplinary problem can impact how your school is viewed by the public.

But there are also times when you need a more formal, well-planned public relations initiative. When you do, remember that the very best plans are developed collaboratively, are flexible and responsive to changing conditions, and provide accurate, useful, and timely information.

Here are some examples of more formal public relations activities used by schools:

- Sharing information about changes in school organization or program.
- Building support for a bond issue to remodel or to make an addition to the school building.
- Providing information on modifications to the extracurricular program, either the athletic program or other activities.
- Building alliances with community educational or social service agencies to support students and their families.

Final Thoughts

Positive communication in education is more important today than ever before. A planned public relations program is a major way to impact not only leaders but also the public. Public relations is a major aspect of determining the success of educational programs and gaining public support.

Final Reflection Questions

What challenge do you face in this particular area of advocacy?

What was the most important thing you learned in this chapter?

How can you apply that lesson in your own situation?

In six months, if you look back on this learning, what would you like to have accomplished?

Q

Quality Relationships

The most important single ingredient in the formula of success is knowing how to get along with people.

—Theodore Roosevelt

Every organization is comprised of all sorts of stakeholders, and those stakeholders often hold very different interests. Building a positive relationship with all stakeholders is key to a successful advocacy effort.

Among those stakeholders, not everyone will be a strong supporter of your initiative. You can think about the people with whom you advocate in a variety of ways, but they often fall into several broad categories.

Categories of Stakeholders

- Champions
- Allies
- Fence-sitters
- Mellow opponents
- Hardcore opponents

Because the interests and the level of support can be so different, it is important to consider a specialized message for each group based on their positions.

Champions

This group often but not always has a background in education and supports innovative approaches to education. They are generally receptive to positive educational changes. Programs that are based on the most rigorous and current scientific evidence are well received by this group. The most effective way to communicate with champions is by sharing research and detailed information about your work. They also enjoy being involved in the decision-making process, even at the initial planning stages.

This group provides you with a strong voice, will assist in media activities, and will be an active coalition of support. They will be key in making personal contacts and speaking before groups.

Ways to Utilize Champions

- Ask them to visit other schools with faculty members to identify new ideas.
- Invite them to coordinate parent-teacher book studies.
- Appoint them to serve on the School Improvement Committee (or other important groups).
- Invite them to write something for the school newsletter.
- Encourage them to monitor your school's social media pages and share their support.
- Introduce them to district leaders, and encourage them to talk about school improvement.
- Identify community groups where they hold membership and ways they can share their support for your school.

Allies

This group is another strong base of support. They may not have the depth of commitment the champions have due to other time or resource commitments, but they play a major support role. Although interested in education, they are simply not as active as champions. They are often a group that will advocate through phone calls, emails, and social media. One of the benefits of allies is the power in numbers. It's important to find ways to involve allies that include providing flexibility.

Ways to Involve Allies

- Ask them to post positive things happening in the school on social media.
- Invite them to contact school board members about issues concerning the school (calls, emails, social media, letters).
- Encourage them to talk with friends, neighbors, and others in the community about your school and its initiatives.
- Provide key talking points (One-Page Fact Sheet) about your plans and other information that they can include in their conversations.
- Offer to meet with them to talk individually about your plans and how they can be supportive.

Fence-Sitters

You have an unusual challenge with fence-sitters. They are often unclear about whether they support any educational issue, and opponents can sway them easily. They respond to solid background information, and it is essential to keep them informed on a regular basis. Building their trust in you as an advocate is essential for this group. Be sure to talk about both the benefits and the costs of any plans. That sort of candor resonates with fence-sitters.

Ways to Address the Needs of Fence-Sitters

- Keep in touch with them consistently, via social media, newsletters, and emails.
- Provide One-Page Fact Sheets (see Chapter X: X Factor: Pitfalls to Avoid) on key issues.
- Ask for their input via surveys, and report back the results.
- Ask champions and allies to share information with fence-sitters.
- Provide accurate assessments of the benefits as well as the costs of plans.
- Meet individually or in small groups to listen to their concerns and provide information.

Mellow Opponents

Opposition from mellow opponents is usually modest. They have a moderate base but rarely want change. This group often has some background in education, and, when you propose changes, they want detailed plans. If you have a positive relationship with them, you can typically gain their support with time and information.

Ways to Address the Needs of Mellow Opponents

- Provide research-based information without educational jargon (One-Page Fact Sheets).
- Provide resources they can research.
- Ask for their input via surveys, and report back the results.
- Provide time for discussion throughout the decision-making process.
- Offer to meet individually or in small groups to listen carefully to their questions and provide detailed information about your plans.

Hardcore Opponents

Hardcore opponents will often oppose any new idea or program and will use any strategy they can to defeat your proposal. You may think about this group as obstructionists. This is your most challenging group because your efforts to advocate for a new idea are likely to be unsuccessful with them.

There are strategies to work with those who oppose you, as discussed in Chapter O: Overcoming Objections. Here are several general strategies that can help you implement change.

Working with Hardcore Opponents

- Build a positive relationship.
- Focus on facts, not personalities. Don't take things personally.
- Utilize your champions and allies to build your case.
- Listen to them, but don't allow them to dominate the discussion.
- Avoid committing to action in response to their objections.
- Offer to meet individually or in small groups to discuss the issue. Often in smaller, more intimate conversation, the objections get diffused.

Groups in Action

Let's look at how these groups interact in a school setting. Ms. Jackson is principal of Harbinger Elementary School. Based on the school's data, it is clear that teachers need to focus more attention on students with disabilities. As Ms. Jackson begins to plan how to best address this with her teachers, she thinks about several of her faculty members.

> **Mr. Dorrell (champion)** is a fifth-grade teacher whose students achieve high test scores. Not only is he committed to his students; he is always looking for new ways to improve his teaching. He is a vocal leader and extremely open to change.
>
> **Ms. Juarez (ally)** teaches kindergarten. She enjoys her job and believes she is becoming a better teacher every year. However, she is very busy with three young children. She is supportive of change but shares her opinion with other individuals rather than speaking up in a meeting.
>
> **Ms. Williams (fence-sitter)** has been teaching for 15 years. She has seen many initiatives come and go, so she usually sits back and waits to see what will happen. She doesn't have strong feelings one way or another about change. You can regularly find her in the faculty workroom asking other teachers what they think.
>
> **Mr. Hemingway (mellow opponent)** has been the media coordinator in the school for 20 years. He is very comfortable in his job and likes stability. His perspective is, "What we are doing works. Why change it?"
>
> **Dr. Morton (hard core opponent)** transferred to the school this year. As a third-grade teacher, she believes she knows what is best—all the time. She is proud that she is the only teacher with a doctorate, and therefore she feels more qualified than anyone else to make a decision. If it's not her idea, it's not a good idea.

Ms. Jackson's next step is to actually design a plan that builds on the strengths of supporters and incorporates ways to involve others that will not derail the plan. Here's how she proceeded.

Teacher	Strategy
Mr. Dorrell, champion	■ Invite to write a post for social media or a column for the newsletter about serving students with disabilities. ■ Ask for assistance in identifying research on best practices for working with students with disabilities.
Ms. Juarez, ally	■ Visit a school recognized for serving students with disabilities and post a report about the visit on social media. ■ Provide One-Page Fact Sheet on the topic with talking points she might use to talk with friends.
Ms. Williams, fence-sitter	■ Invite to serve on planning committee. ■ Provide background information on serving students with disabilities. ■ Ask for her input and suggestions about how to proceed.
Mr. Hemingway, mellow opponent	■ Share a One-Page Fact Sheet on the importance of services to students with disabilities. ■ Talk individually with him about the issue while listening for areas of concern or support. ■ Provide additional information to build on support or about areas of concern.
Dr. Morton, hardcore opponent	■ Visit classroom and talk with him about his concerns. ■ Listen to objections, and identify clues about the reasons for resistance. ■ Provide additional information about concerns, and acknowledge both benefits and costs of plan.

Final Thoughts

Understanding the various types of stakeholders can help you be a better advocate. In order to implement positive change in your school or district, you'll want to use strategies to most effectively work with each group.

Final Reflection Questions

What challenge do you face in this particular area of advocacy?

What was the most important thing you learned in this chapter?

How can you apply that lesson in your own situation?

In six months, if you look back on this learning, what would you like to have accomplished?

R

Resistance to Change

Resistance to change should be a thing of the past if we could develop growth mindsets and create organizations with growth cultures.

—Paul Gibbons

There is an old saying: "The only person who likes change is a baby with a wet diaper." Each of us has likely dealt with someone who was not supportive of a proposed change. Successful advocates understand that reluctance can be part of the process and use that reluctance, along with the issues people raise, to clarify and focus the planned change.

Ways People Respond to Change

People respond to change in one of several ways. Approximately 5% are early adopters and are eager to embrace almost any innovation. Another 5% will never adopt change; nothing can get them to embrace an innovation. The remainder are people who may be reluctant but who can be moved toward support if provided sufficient time and information. In this chapter, we will focus on that 90%. How can you help those who are reluctant to change become part of positive progress?

Reasons for Resisting Change

Think of the last time you wanted to implement a change in your school or district. You probably heard a variety of responses similar to the following.

Comments Resisting Change

> I don't see why we need to do this.
>
> You [the principal] already made up your mind to change.
>
> My opinion doesn't count.
>
> This is just one more thing to do.
>
> How does this relate to what we are already doing?
>
> We've tried this before and it didn't work.

People generally resist change for one of two reasons. They don't see the value of the change, or they do not believe they can be successful with the change. Each of the preceding comments fits into one of those categories. As an advocate, it is imperative to understand these two reasons in order to respond accordingly.

Value

Students sometimes ask, "Why do we need to learn this?" Similarly, stakeholders sometimes ask, "Why do we need to do this?" The question may be spoken or unspoken, directed to you, or discussed in the parking lot, but it is always at the forefront of any proposed change. To support an innovation, stakeholders must understand the value of the change.

As you think about how the innovation you are considering is of value, it's important to remember Maslow's hierarchy. When you adopt a new innovation, you may find that many employees, even those with high levels of success, revert to a lower level. They are concerned about basic needs (materials, training, schedule, etc.) and must understand how those will be met before they can address the higher levels of the hierarchy.

Maslow's Needs

Need as Identified by Maslow	Examples of Employees' Needs	Examples of Parents' Needs
Aesthetic need (self-actualization)	Attention to the needs of students first	Will there be a detrimental effect on my child?
Need for understanding	Focus on the developmental needs of students	How do I go about supporting the school and my child in this new venture?

Need for knowledge	Professional development:
	    Program models
	    Planning skills
	    Curriculum
	    Instructional strategies
	    Diversity issues
	    Assessment strategies
		Do I have sufficient information to decide on the proposal plan?
		How will I be informed about the program and its implementation?
		Where do I go to get more information about this plan?

Esteem needs Belonging needs	Will I be successful? Will I be valued? Will I fit in? How do the new social and work norms align with my beliefs?	Will my child be successful? Will my child continue to be valued? How will my child succeed in the new plan?
Security needs	Where will I be working? Where will my room or office be located? What will my work look like? Who's making these decisions?	What will happen to my child? Will my child be safe?

(continued on the next page)

Need as Identified by Maslow	Examples of Employees' Needs	Examples of Parents' Needs
Survival needs	Will I continue to have a job? Will I have the skills for the job? Will I have sufficient and appropriate materials?	Will my child be successful? Will my child have the skills to succeed?

Source: Adapted from Maslow (1968).

Success

The second facet of resistance is the desire to succeed. Most people have high competence needs, and they believe they are successful in their current work. Any change is viewed through a lens of how the person can continue to be successful. Therefore, you should provide appropriate support to help develop the skills to be successful with new innovation. Make sure teachers and other staff have the knowledge and skills to successfully implement your plan.

How to Respond

Despite the appearance of stubbornness, most people don't resist just to resist; they resist because they lack information about an innovation or because they don't have adequate time to embrace it. Time and information are the two keys to overcoming resistance. First, you must provide time for most of those involved to adopt and learn about the innovation. Second, you will need to provide sufficient information about how the innovation will impact people's work. Remember, everyone needs to feel successful. You can use five strategies to smooth the transition process and overcome the resistance to change.

Strategy 1: Build Relationships and Involve People

The first strategy for overcoming resistance to change is to build relationships with all stakeholders and involve them in the proposed change. During this step, it's important to identify everyone who will be affected by the change. It's easy to overlook someone who is not directly involved in a project but whose support will be critical in the future. Ensure their cooperation by involving them early.

Possible Stakeholders or Constituent Groups

- Families
- Community members
- Community service agencies (e.g., medical, mental health)
- Citizens without children in the schools
- Teachers and other school personnel
- Teachers from feeder schools
- City agencies (e.g., Recreation Department)

Strategy 2: Establish a Common Base of Information

As you work with all constituency groups, establish a common base of information for the proposed change. One of stumbling blocks to progress is a lack of information; therefore, be sure everyone has a sufficient knowledge base to discuss and move ahead with the project. Although this can happen through a large group discussion, such as in a faculty meeting, it is usually more effective to provide multiple opportunities for conversation in smaller groups prior to a discussion with the entire faculty. In large groups, some voices dominate the discussion, and it is easy to miss important information from people less willing to speak.

- Individually, make notes about current conditions in your school community. Identify critical issues and the evidence to support their inclusion.
- With colleagues, discuss the conditions you identified, develop a ranking or priority for the concerns, cite the evidence, and agree on trends affecting your school community. Discuss and identify the implications of each item for schools. The following chart is helpful in that process.

Concerns-Based Discussion Chart

Concern	Ranking	Evidence	Implications

Strategy 3: Provide a Clear, Concrete Result

This strategy is often assumed and therefore may be overlooked. In order to overcome resistance to change, stakeholders need to see a clear, defined outcome. You should always be able to answer one question: "If we are successful implementing _____, we will know it because we will see _____." In other words, what would success look like? This does not mean you must develop the vision yourself without any input; the most lasting visions are shared ones. However, for any proposed change, it is important to have a clear vision and to share that vision with all constituent groups.

Strategy 4: Have a Structure That Supports Success

Fourth, you need to build a structure that supports success. This does not mean you must know every step prior to implementation. However, you do need a way to clearly identify each step, a proposed time frame, roles and responsibilities, and necessary resources. Using a Process Chart such as the one that follows is helpful in ensuring that all participants understand each step and their roles in the process. Remember that your structure should incorporate the elements of value and success, such as providing appropriate professional development that will help teachers feel more successful with the proposed change.

Process/Change

Strategy	Time Frame	Person(s) Responsible	Resources Needed

Strategy 5: Focus and Refocus the Conversation

Finally, keep the conversation focused. It is easy, particularly in a large group discussion, to become distracted by personal agendas. In a recent workshop, a leadership team was planning a remediation class for at-risk learners. Two teachers began to argue about classroom space and their own scheduling preferences. As previously noted, people revert to lower levels of Maslow's hierarchy when they are concerned about change. In this instance, the group had already developed a solution to both those issues, but the two teachers continued to complain. The principal reminded the group of the rationale for the remediation classes: to positively affect student learning for their neediest students, particularly second-language learners, by providing additional time for learning. She reframed the conversation, and the group was able to move forward. In addition to having a vision for change, you must continually keep that vision as a focus. And at times you will need to use the vision to refocus the conversation.

Helpful Ideas for Communicating When Conflict Is Present

- Share data and descriptions, not value judgments or interpretations.
- Use active listening skills.
- Focus on the present, not what has been or might be.
- Agree when those of a different viewpoint are right.
- Own your ideas and feelings; use "I" as much as possible.
- Guard against too much openness.
- Make constructive use of silence; provide and demand time to think.
- Delay making judgments or decisions.
- Explain, do not defend.
- Be sensitive to nonverbal clues and messages.
- Recognize and request rewording of questions that have no answers, that are rhetorical, or that include commands or directions.
- Avoid the use of superlatives and absolutes ("most," "best," "always," "never").
- Assume the motives of others are honorable.
- Discourage preaching and teaching behaviors.

Final Thoughts

Finally, remember that overcoming resistance to change is possible. The vast majority of those you are advocating to can and will respond appropriately if they see the value of the innovation and if they believe they will be successful. It is your job to help them do so.

Final Reflection Questions

What challenge do you face in this particular area of advocacy?
What was the most important thing you learned in this chapter?
How can you apply that lesson in your own situation?
In six months, if you look back on this learning, what would you like to have accomplished?

S

Successful Negotiations

Almost everything we do involves some form of negotiation. That's true in our work at school with teachers, staff, students, and families. It's also true in our personal lives. For example, if you have a teenager, you know you are always negotiating over things like chores, curfews, and money. Negotiation is more than resolving employee issues or collective bargaining. Successful negotiating involves listening to others and respecting and valuing their ideas and opinions, even when we don't agree.

The same is true when you're advocating for your school. Almost always, advocating means working with partners to achieve desired outcomes. While the formal term might be "negotiation," which may seem somewhat adversarial, what we really mean is working with others to achieve our shared goals. This approach strengthens our relationship with our partners. In this chapter, we'll focus specifically on the stages of the "negotiation" process, as well as strategies and tips for successful negotiating.

So what is negotiation? It is a way that people share their views and settle differences. To meet our goals and achieve success, we must have the ability to balance many different personalities and points of view. The most successful negotiators bring a collection of interpersonal and communication skills to any negotiations.

Interpersonal and Communication Skills for Negotiation

Interpersonal Skills	Communication Skills
■ Friendliness ■ Smiling face ■ Open or neutral arms ■ Loose, rather than tense, body language	■ Clarity ■ Brevity ■ Needs-based ■ Use of open-ended questions ■ Ability to listen

Stages of Negotiation

Conflicts and disagreements arise as different people with different views and different backgrounds meet and discuss issues.

Here's a six-point negotiation design suggested by Skillsyouneed.com (n.d.).

1. **Preparation**—Complete your homework prior to any meeting or call. It is essential to know all the benefits and challenges of an issue, as well as information about the person with whom you'll be talking.
2. **Discussion**—Always make sure there is an open discussion of all sides of an issue. Every issue has its benefits and costs. Be open in the discussion and respectful of other points of view.
3. **Clarification of goals**—Be clear on your priorities, as well as the priorities of the person with whom you are working.
4. **Negotiate toward a positive outcome**—Negotiation is a process, and compromise is necessary. Working toward an outcome that can be described beneficial to all parties is important.
5. **Agreement**—When you finish your conversation, be sure to agree on what was said, including both sides' perspectives. Restate the agreement, and put it in writing.
6. **Implementation**—Always have a plan to implement the agreement.

Short Process

On occasion, you may have a crisis or only a short time to negotiate or deal with a specific problem. In that case, you may want to consider this three-stage process suggested by Changing Minds (n.d.).

Short Process

> 1. **Open**—Say what you want.
> 2. **Bargain**—Hammer out the deal.
> 3. **Close**—Agree and exchange.

In this case, you compress the original six steps, but, given the shorter amount of time, you focus on these three points. For example, when meeting with a local businessperson, you might have a conversation like this:

Sample Three-Step Process

Ms. Wilson, thank you for giving me five minutes of your time today. I know you are busy, so I'll keep this short. We are expanding our literacy program in our school, and want to provide audio books for our students who are struggling. I'd like you to consider asking your employees to read and record books for us. We would provide all materials, and they would be able to do the work at their convenience. Would that be of interest to you?

Yes, we are always interested in supporting the schools. But I'm concerned about how much time it will take.

We have used the process with other groups, and it takes between 10 and 20 minutes for each book. Do you think your employees might be able to do that?

I think so. That isn't much time.

Would you be willing to ask them to participate and distribute information about the program?

Yes, I can do that.

Would you also be willing to find a volunteer within the company who can work with us to coordinate the program? Perhaps someone who has organizational skills?

I think we can. I have someone in mind, and, because her daughter is at your school, I think she would be willing.

Great. It sounds like we have a plan. We will provide all materials to your employees who choose to participate in our plan to record audio books for students. You will ask them to participate and distribute information we provide, and you will find someone who can coordinate the efforts with us.

Yes, that's right.

Great. Thank you for your time, and I'll be back in touch.

Notice how, in the short conversation, the advocate chunked the tasks? Rather than asking for everything at once, he broke it down and gained a commitment for each step. Sometimes, we are so excited about our plan, we rush into a full description, and it is overwhelming to our potential partner. One thing to remember: Sometimes, despite your best efforts to work together, you cannot come to an agreement. It's important to keep in mind that you may simply need to shift your advocacy efforts.

Strategies for Successful Negotiations

In addition to the stages of negotiation, four strategies can help you negotiate, or advocate, for your position.

First, don't be afraid to ask for what you want. Assertiveness is a positive word, although we don't always think so. Barbara points out that when she was a teacher, she felt like compliance was the norm, so she wasn't comfortable advocating for an issue. It's important to encourage assertiveness, while avoiding aggressiveness. Assertiveness speaks with confidence, not anger, and it is an effective tool in the negotiating process.

Next, always listen. There's an old saying, "Nature gave us two ears and one mouth so that we listen twice as much as speak." How often do we do that? When we listen, we can adjust our message, and we are more likely to accomplish our outcome. Asking a variety of open-ended questions will help you in this process.

If possible, don't be in a hurry unless you don't have a choice. Negotiations usually take time, especially if you are attempting to garner support for a long-term issue or project. If we rush into a decision, we usually regret it, and if we push our stakeholder to make a quick decision, she may walk away. In fact, there's some evidence that taking time to think about a plan can actually lead to a stronger, more viable result.

Fourth, show the other person how his needs will be met. The ultimate goal of a negotiation is that both sides leave feeling positive. In order for that to happen, you'll need to demonstrate how the stakeholder will benefit from the recommendations.

Effective Negotiation Skills

Having read this chapter, you probably thought about the skills that are necessary to be successful. After all, negotiation is simply one form of advocacy. Luanne Kelchner provides a set of skills that every negotiator should possess.

Top Ten Effective Negotiation Skills

1. Problem analysis
2. Preparation
3. Active listening
4. Emotional control
5. Verbal communication
6. Collaboration and teamwork
7. Problem solving
8. Decision making ability
9. Interpersonal skills
10. Ethics and reliability

Source: Kelchner (n.d.).

Final Thoughts

Negotiating is an important part of the advocacy process. Negotiation is the heart of achieving your goal. Working through the stages of negotiation and using skills and strategies to help you be more effective will assist in your advocacy efforts.

Final Reflection Questions

What challenge do you face in this particular area of advocacy?

What was the most important thing you learned in this chapter?

How can you apply that lesson in your own situation?

In six months, if you look back on this learning, what would you like to have accomplished?

Time, Friend or Foe?

How did it get so late so soon?

—Dr. Seuss

> A special thank-you to Dr. Frank Buck, author of *Get Organized! Time Management for School Leaders*, for writing this chapter.

Advocates are passionate people. Regardless of how we feel on a personal level, we are only effective when we can get others to share at least a portion of our passion. The job is often difficult. It's seldom accomplished through one phone call, meeting, or message. Instead, we achieve success through a series of well-planned steps mapped across time.

Talk to people in any field about what keeps them from getting their important work done, and you are likely to hear a common theme: lack of time. They approach time as a foe to be battled. In this chapter, you will learn how to turn time into a friend.

See All of Your Choices

Time management is about making choices. We live in a connected world in which we are bombarded with information. The temptation is to respond to the latest input. Do you find yourself exhausted at the end of the day, yet feel you accomplished little? Do you sense you are farther behind than you were when the day began? If so, you may be a victim of chasing rabbits when you could be hunting tigers.

Adopt a digital task list. Toodledo, Wunderlist, Asana, Todoist, and Remember the Milk are but a few of the web-based task managers. Each offers a companion app for your mobile devices. Get rid of the sticky notes, scraps of paper, and assorted memos pads. Consolidate it all in one place. Then, and only then, you gain a sense of how much you have committed to do versus the time in which you have to do it.

When you get everything in front of you, you start to see patterns. You see how you can batch related tasks and handle them more quickly. You also start to see tasks that you could delegate to other people while you save your time for the tasks that only you can perform. Finally, you start to see that some of what you have on your list simply has to go.

The key is to get it all in front of you. When you can see all of your choices, you start to make better choices.

Establish Priorities

Plan your day by looking at your list. Rather than starting the day by conjuring a list out of your head, start with a list of predefined work. Each task is added thoughtfully. Each task remains on the list until you either complete it or decide it no longer has value.

Start the day by looking at the list and putting the tasks in order. Look for the "Fab Five." If you were to accomplish only five tasks today, what would they be? If you truly accomplish your Fab Five regularly, you will see major accomplishments in your role as an advocate and in every role in your life.

Maintain Focus

Interruptions are part of our lives. Their presence represents the valuableness of our input into collaborative projects. However, their frequency is often to blame for failure to accomplish what we want in a given day. How can we maintain our focus and still be available to other people?

Resist the temptation to jump on a new task as soon as you end that phone call or conversation with a drop-in visitor. A better use of your time is to record the task on your list and get back to the work you were doing before the interruption. The incoming tasks will grow during the day, and you can probably handle an entire batch of them in less time than doing them one by one as they present themselves.

Are you the source of interruption for others? Do you find yourself picking up the phone or walking down the hall to ask a question and repeat the process five minutes later when you think of another one? Use your task list to trap those questions so that you do not forget them. When someone calls or drops in for an impromptu meeting, handle the items you had accumulated on your list for them.

When the subject is interruptions, we are often our own worst enemies. How often do you interrupt yourself from important work to check your email for the 37th time today or see what has happened in the world of Twitter in the last five minutes? Make the task list attractive. Word the items clearly so that you know exactly what to do on each task. With the Fab Five at the top of the list, your task list should be the hub of your day.

Master Follow-Up

Think about the advocates who have been wildly successful in getting their voices heard. How many of them do so in isolation? If you are leading an advocacy movement, you have others who are helping spread the message. You routinely delegate responsibilities. How will you keep up with which people have come through on their assignments?

When you assign a task to someone face-to-face, over the phone, or via voicemail, add a task to your list. When would you like to be reminded that you had delegated that task so that you can follow up? The answer to that question becomes the due date of the task. On the prescribed day, you will have that reminder. Good digital task lists include a search feature. Searching for a person's name will reveal all of the tasks involving him.

Understand Timing and the Media

You want to be able to tell the story of the topic that is near and dear to you. The media can help you tell that story to a much larger audience. One of the keys to working with the media is timing. How can you link your cause to an already existing media event?

Does your cause relate to a popular New Year's resolution? See if you can schedule an appearance on a local television or radio talk show in early January. Even better, is your cause associated with a nationally recognized week or day? If so, your particular expertise becomes more newsworthy.

Plan ahead. Research which people you need to contact at each media outlet. Prepare your pitch and supporting materials in such a way that it will grab the interest of others in just a few seconds. Be prepared to leave messages and follow up as needed. Everything takes longer than you think.

See the Big Things and the Small Things

Successful advocates know that a single phone call, email, or face-to-face conversation seldom brings about change. In fact, if the conversation is with a top decision maker, it may well be preceded by any number of tasks that made that conversation possible. The advocacy puzzle often includes many parts. In addition to your role as an advocate, you are also holding down a full-time job, serving in civic organizations, and fulfilling your role as a spouse or parent. How can you keep all of the balls in the air?

In *Get Organized: Time Management for School Leaders*, Frank Buck explains it this way:

> A juggler keeps a number of balls in the air by *giving each one a little attention on a regular basis*. The juggler knows just how many objects he has in the air, where each one is, when attention is needed, and how much attention is needed. We need to know exactly the same thing about each of our projects.

A famous Alvin Toffler quote reminds us, "You've got to think about big things while you're doing small things, so that all the small things go in the right direction." In your efforts as an advocate, most of what you will do will be small things. You will read an article, compose an email, talk to a person on the street. Individually, all the small things seem insignificant. Together, they are the stuff that moves mountains. As you check off the boxes on your list, never forget the bigger "why."

An equally famous Helen Keller quote tells us, "While they were saying it couldn't be done, it was done." When that cause for which you fought has been won, you will look back over your efforts. You will think of all the tasks you handled, the way you followed through, the focus you maintained, and the way you may made the best choices of all the available tasks. You took what was important to you and made it important to others. And you did it all through the dimension of time.

Decades ago, Julie Andrews closed her television variety show each week with a song entitled "Time Is My Friend." Through your efforts, you realize that, with the right skills, time is also your friend.

Final Thoughts

For leaders, the idea of being an advocate can be overwhelming. How do you fit advocacy into a busy day? These tips on time management provide proven strategies not only for managing your advocacy efforts but also for controlling your use of time.

Final Reflection Questions

What challenge do you face in this particular area of advocacy?

What was the most important thing you learned in this chapter?

How can you apply that lesson in your own situation?

In six months, if you look back on this learning, what would you like to have accomplished?

U

Up-to-Date on the Issues

Successful advocates are proactive, not reactive. They understand that it is important to stay current on trends affecting their students and their school. This chapter will discuss strategies for staying current and then suggest some current issues that will continue to impact schools.

Gary Marx of Educational Research Service (2006) suggests that insightful leaders recognize that things change and that they need to stay informed and up-to-date on issues and trends. Interestingly, Marx suggests that the more difficult issue may be deciding what to work on rather than the process of change itself. This requires changing old habits and perspectives of the role of the principal.

Four Key Shifts

Marx identified several shifts that are fundamentally changing schools. He encourages leaders to be attentive to those shifts and how they impact both schooling and leadership.

1. Successful leaders are not solitary figures at the top of the organization but rather embrace a more horizontal leadership team. No single person can possibly know everything, and the need for multiple conceptions of leadership and pathways to leadership is critical. That means collaboration with others in your school, in your district, and in the larger school community.

2. Access to information is changing the way students learn and teachers teach. The integration of technology as a tool for teaching and learning will only continue to accelerate. Staying current and up-to-date on the latest technology and its application to learning is critical.
3. Schools are interconnected with all facets of the community and the world. It is essential to recognize the connections with families, community leaders, and economic, political, and social systems. Effective advocates build partnerships with the larger school community and use those partnerships as opportunities to advocate for their students and their school.
4. The most successful leaders will be those that are able to work with others to create a shared vision for the future. Rather than perpetuating the past, they will enthusiastically embrace future trends, acknowledging that those trends will shape the future of their school regardless of personal preferences.

Because schools are connected to their larger community and the world, leaders must constantly monitor changes in their community and in the larger context in which schools function. This will guide your advocacy efforts.

Responding to These Shifts

Underlying each of these shifts is the fact that change will occur. It is a constant part of our lives. Skillful advocates do several things to assure that they are current and up-to-date on issues that may impact their school.

1. **Analyze the environment**—Scan the environment in which your school exists—district, community, state, nation, and world. What are the issues that affect your school, and what issues affect the world more broadly? These trends and issues often emerge as important.
2. **Monitor changes in the environment**—Read voraciously, talk with a broad selection of people in your community, stay current with trends at the state and national level.
3. **Identify the factors impacting your school**—Look beyond the traditional educational factors (good teachers, money) and consider emerging issues like the maturing of the community, the ability to acquire and use technology, the ability to respond to changing conditions.
4. **Challenge your own assumptions**—After identifying some of the assumptions you hold about your school and its environment, test them by assessing their degree of certainty (high-medium-low) and the level of impact (high-medium-low). Assumptions play an important role in constructing a future, and they should be as reliable as possible.

5. **Develop a vision of a viable future**—Consider the issues you think will emerge to impact your school and the factors you identified that are critical to success. Develop a vision of a future different from current circumstances. Creation of several alternatives is even better. Then identify how you can advocate with others in your school community for your school to succeed in this environment.
6. **Develop an advocacy plan**—Identify specific steps that can be taken to respond to the anticipated future. Strengthen your relationship with partners to share information, secure resources, and create your vision. See Chapter D: Designing an Advocacy Plan for more detail.
7. **Implement plans and monitor progress**—Once you launch your plan, be sure to gather data about progress. Use this data to add richness and context to your advocacy efforts.

Although it is impossible to predict the future, several trends are likely to continue to impact schools. We wouldn't pretend that this list includes everything that may emerge but at the time of publication these issues are important to monitor.

Anticipated Trends

1. Demands at the state and national levels for greater accountability for improved student learning will increase. Educators will be pressed to be more successful with all students. How do you advocate for appropriate indicators of success, indicators that align with your instructional program?
2. The demographics of students in schools will continue to change. Schools will be expected to provide a high-quality educational program for groups that have often been underserved by schools. How will you advocate for the professional development and resources needed to serve every student?
3. Stable or declining resources will characterize the educational environment. Schools will be expected to be more efficient as well as more effective. How can you advocate with state and federal leaders to assure that schools have the resources they need to succeed?
4. Technology is constantly changing, and schools must adapt to those changes. How do you plan to advocate for your students to have access to the latest technology so that they can develop the skills needed for success in the workplace?

(Continued)

(*Continued*)

5. For decades we've been talking about choice, and in most states it has become a reality. Families have a wide variety of options for their children's schooling. How will you respond in a choice environment to advocate for your school and to share your school's successes with your school community?
6. A major national trend is the decline in the number of college students interested in teaching or school leadership. If those trends persist, schools will face shortages of both teachers and leaders. How might you advocate with your own district to make teaching an attractive option for college graduates? How will you advocate with state and national leaders to assure that prospective teachers see teaching as a viable career option, one with the salary and benefits that can compete with lucrative private sector jobs?

How Do You Respond?

We work with dozens of school leaders every year, and we appreciate the complexity of their work. From these principals, we've learned that school leaders can do several critical things to respond to emerging issues and to build their skills as advocates.

- **Build trust and respect**—Skillful leaders recognize that when trust is present, teachers and principals can confront complex and difficult issues. They are able to work together to construct solutions that reflect the school's priorities.
- **Stay true to your core values and beliefs**—Never compromise your integrity by acting in ways that are contrary to your personal vision. Always work to align your work with those values and beliefs that guide your life.
- **Be intellectually curious**—Read a lot, and think a lot about current and emerging trends. Be open to ways to improve your school even when things are going well.
- **Challenge the regularities of schooling**—Be comfortable questioning past practices, especially the things that are taken for granted in schools. A good friend of Ron's stated that principals should always be looking for the perfect solution, all the while knowing no perfect solution exists.
- **Build bridges to families and communities**—No school leader is ever successful without the deep and abiding trust of the families who send

their children to their school. Similarly, the community must trust that your values and priorities are focused on the students' best interests.

- **Hire only the best teachers and other employees**—Principals want confidence about the quality of teaching and learning in their school. That means that only the best should ever be hired, and principals should be comfortable deferring a decision until the appropriate candidate is available.
- **Cultivate a critical friend, someone outside your school or outside education**—Such a friend can provide a fresh perspective on issues you face. They can help you think about how you will continue to advocate for your students and your school.
- **Enjoy what you do**—Relish the impact that school leaders have on the education of students in their school. But when the enjoyment fades, find ways to reinvigorate your passion or move your career in alternate ways.

Final Thoughts

One thing is constant, and that is change. Schools and school communities change a little bit each and every day as new students arrive, families move to your community, faculty retire, or issues emerge that shape the expectations and demands on your school. Skillful leaders understand that dynamic and anticipate the way those issues may impact their school. They recognize the importance of utilizing successful advocacy skills to build and strengthen relationships with their school community.

Final Reflection Questions

What challenge do you face in this particular area of advocacy?

What was the most important thing you learned in this chapter?

How can you apply that lesson in your own situation?

In six months, if you look back on this learning, what would you like to have accomplished?

V

Vision: Personal and Shared

The very essence of leadership is [that] you have a vision. It's got to be a vision you articulate clearly and forcefully on every occasion. You can't blow an uncertain trumpet.

—Theodore Hesburgh

Effective advocates have a vision of what they want for their school and for the way new initiatives will support that vision. Use that principle to develop a clear vision for your advocacy efforts

A Personal Vision for Advocacy

Your personal vision for advocacy consists of the most fundamental beliefs you hold about your life, about your work, and about your relationships with people and how all those beliefs impact your advocacy efforts. As a result, it is not easy to write a personal vision statement. Before you can work with others to develop a shared vision, it is important to have your own personal vision.

Four Steps to Developing a Personal Advocacy Vision Statement

- **Step 1**: Think about your school or district. Make a list of what you would like to achieve to make improvements. Describe what it looks like and feels like.
- **Step 2**: Consider the following things about what you have written: relationships, personal interests, and community. Consider how each factor impacts your role as an advocate.
- **Step 3**: Develop a list of priorities. Identify the most important. Once this is done, review the list and rank the entries from most to least important. Remove the least important. Rerank if appropriate. Check for relevance with your earlier list. Eliminate any item that is not relevant.
- **Step 4**: Use the items from the first three steps to develop a personal vision advocacy statement. Review and edit the statement as often as needed until you believe it accurately reflects your commitment to more rigorous schools and classrooms.

Source: Adapted from Williamson & Blackburn (2016).

Shared Vision: The Key

Having a personal vision for your school is critical, but the most successful advocates are those who recognize the importance of a shared vision, a vision developed collaboratively with stakeholders and one that is embraced and supported by each of those stakeholder groups.

Assessing Facilitators and Barriers to Involvement

At a basic level, a willingness to participate in advocacy efforts is a great facilitator or motivator. Similarly, not wanting to be involved is a clear barrier. For some of your stakeholders, the barrier may be circumstance dependent. For example, a faculty member with a new baby may not have the time or energy to take on an advocacy role right now. However, the same teacher may be more than willing to support your efforts later or in other ways. We worked with a school whose faculty wanted to advocate for more parental involvement. Some teachers were willing to take on leadership roles, but a first-year teacher was concerned. She was already overwhelmed, and taking on new responsibilities simply seemed to be too much. The other teachers came up with a plan where the first-year teacher could be involved with a minimal commitment.

From a broader perspective, there are a variety of facilitators and barriers to involvement for you to consider prior to asking individuals to participate.

Facilitators and Barriers

Facilitators	Barriers
■ There is adequate time to meet, talk about rigor, plan, implement, and assess current efforts. Lots of time may be required initially to get started. ■ There is a clear understanding of the areas/topics that the group can address. ■ Appropriate, ongoing professional development is available for all stakeholders, including conflict management and decision-making skills. ■ Participants are accountable and responsible. ■ Technical assistance is available. ■ The principal offers comfort and support.	■ Little or no professional development on collaborative work is provided. ■ Limits of decision-making authority are unclear or undefined. ■ Principal directs and tells rather than guides. ■ Only the principal or superintendent is held accountable for decisions. ■ Group does not have power to make "real" decisions and gets mired in unimportant details.

Shared Vision Tool 1: Vision Letters

Now, it's time to build a shared vision with your stakeholders. The first step is to have them develop personal visions for advocacy and then to share those in order to develop a collective vision.

Ask your stakeholders to imagine that it is a year from today. In retrospect, the year turned out to be their best year ever in terms of advocacy efforts, one that far exceeded their expectations. Now ask them to write a letter or email addressing the year. What successes occurred with advocacy? How did you accomplish those successes? How were others involved in your advocacy efforts? Next, ask the stakeholders to share their letters with someone else in the group. Use this as a starting point to discuss the shared vision for advocacy.

Sample Vision Letter

Dear Marissa,

This year, I decided to focus on advocating for issues in my school. I think I had done this informally before, but now I made a specific plan and carried through. Throughout the year, I identified issues that were important to my school, such as expanding our technology instruction, supporting our struggling readers, and increasing the rigor throughout all our classes.

After I identified my issues, I drafted a list of ways to advocate for these changes to all stakeholders—teachers, parents, business partners, and district office personnel. Then I began to talk informally to those stakeholders to see whether anyone else was on board with these changes and would support my advocacy efforts. So many people volunteered, I was amazed.

We worked together as a group to prioritize our issues, identify specific action steps, and divide responsibilities among the members of the group. One thing that surprised me was that they came up with ideas I had not considered. Throughout the year, they talked to other people, held information meetings and professional development, and asked for financial support for our technology program.

The results were amazing. By the end of the year, 100% of our teachers were committed to supporting our struggling readers, increasing rigor in all classes, and expanding our technology instruction. Not only were they committed, they had already begun to implement what they could, such as instructional strategies for scaffolding reading and for increasing rigor. Two teachers wrote a grant for our technology program, one posted a project on DonorsChoose, and a group of teachers and students presented to the School Board about our needs.

I learned that advocacy is truly an action—one that is critical to effectively impact your school. And it works best when you collaborate with others to make change happen.

Thanks for your support,

Pete

Shared Vision Tool 2: Hot Air Balloon

Another activity you can use as you develop a shared vision is the Hot Air Balloon Vision Activity.

Hot Air Balloon Vision Activity

Ask each person on the team to list his or her ideas individually and then to share them with the group. Finally, collaborate to create a shared list that everyone can support. Do this for each of the two steps.

Step One

Imagine you are in a hot air balloon high in the sky over our school/district.

You are looking down at your educational programs.

What do you see? What can you hear?

Step Two

It is five years from now, and you have returned in your hot air balloon.

Things have changed, and it is now the most effective educational program in our state.

What do you see? What do you hear?

Once you have completed both steps, compare the shared lists. Ask stakeholders to identify what they want to change or improve in order to reach their ideal vision.

Final Thoughts

A vision is what shapes and guides your work. It can be a significant motivator for achieving your goals. Create a personal vision for advocacy, but work with others to build a shared vision. This process will assist you in your advocacy efforts.

Final Reflection Questions

What challenge do you face in this particular area of advocacy?
What was the most important thing you learned in this chapter?
How can you apply that lesson in your own situation?
In six months, if you look back on this learning, what would you like to have accomplished?

W

Working with Local, State, and National Governance

I am not anxious to be the loudest voice or the most popular. But I would like to think that at a crucial moment, I was an effective voice of the voiceless, an effective hope of the hopeless.

—Whitney Young

Government, from the local to the national levels, impacts all of us and our schools. Almost all schools report to local school boards. State legislatures and the U.S. Congress and other government agencies pass laws and issue regulations that impact schools. At each level, there is an opportunity for advocacy. To be an effective advocate, it is essential that the elements of the governance structure and the function of each part be understood.

Always remember that legislators and employees of governmental agencies are often generalists and need explicit, factual input from citizens.

Elements of Governance

To be an effective advocate, it is essential that we understand the elements of governance structure and function. Basically there are three levels of governance—federal, state, and local—as well as three branches of governance—executive, legislative, and judicial.

Three Levels of Governance

1. Federal
2. State
3. Local

Federal

Education is primarily a state and local responsibility in the United States. The Tenth Amendment to the Constitution leaves the administration of education to the states. However, after the launch of Sputnik in 1957, there was concern about the quality of math, science, and foreign language instruction in the United States. Congress passed the Elementary and Secondary Education Act that included grants to schools to improve instruction in these three subjects. These grants, called "Eisenhower Grants," were among the first expenditure of federal dollars for K–12 public schools. As with most things, with the funds came rules and regulations for the use of those funds.

The Elementary and Secondary Education Act was reauthorized regularly. Occasionally, the name was changed and the focus modified. This occurred most notably when Congress changed the name to No Child Left Behind (NCLB) in 2001. No Child Left Behind included explicit direction about use of funds and the achievement targets for students. Just recently the law was rewritten and is now the Every Student Succeeds Act (ESSA) of 2015. This rewrite loosens the federal rules and provides states with greater flexibility in the use of the funds.

In 1980, Congress established the Department of Education as a Cabinet-level agency. When Bob attended an open hearing in Washington, D.C., on establishing the role of the federal government in education, one of the key pieces of information shared was that the role of the federal government would be to supplement states' efforts, not to supplant them.

Today, the Department operates programs that touch on every area and level of education. In addition to monitoring implementation of ESSA, the department monitors a variety of grant programs like the GEAR UP program to promote college readiness and access and programs like the Individuals with Disabilities Education Improvement Act (IDEIA).

State

It is states and communities, as well as public and private organizations of all kinds, that establish schools, develop curricula, and determine requirements for enrollment and graduation. The Tenth Amendment gives this right to states.

The Tenth Amendment

> The powers not delegated to the United States by the Constitution, nor prohibited by it to the states, are reserved to the states respectively, or to the people.

State legislatures pass laws that regulate schools within their boundaries and create agencies that help to manage schools. Every state has some form of a state department of education. State departments have the responsibility to write the rules and regulations to implement, at the state and local level, laws like ESSA and IDEIA. In addition, they gather performance data about student learning and are responsible for licensing and credentialing school employees.

Local

Local control refers to (1) the governing and management of public schools by elected or appointed representatives serving on governing bodies, such as school boards or school committees, that are located in the communities served by the schools, and (2) the degree to which local leaders, institutions, and governing bodies can make independent or autonomous decisions about the governance and operation of public schools.

Local control is based on the belief that those individuals nearest to the students and most knowledgeable about education make the best decision for the local community. Academic and management decisions reflect the community values and norms. School boards comprised of locally elected members offer the best approach to excellence in education because of their more intimate knowledge of each school district and the community it serves.

Each state differs in the local organization of governance, such as counties, towns, cities, and parishes, and their schools reflect this difference. For example, in some states, local boards of education have taxing authority to add funding to local schools. In all states, local school districts and boards of education are agents of the state and can be merged or dissolved as the state wishes. In many states, there is a movement to reduce the number of school districts due to the cost of sustaining separate administrative systems, transportation systems, and separate sets of employees.

Three Branches of Governance

Three Branches of Governance

> 1. Legislative
> 2. Executive
> 3. Judicial

The state legislative branch is made up of the two houses of Congress—the Senate and the House of Representatives—except in Nebraska where there is a unicameral legislature. The primary duty of the legislative branch is to make laws. Laws are prepared, submitted, discussed, and voted on in Congress, or the legislature, in the state.

The function of the executive branch is to administer the law. The president or governor approves and carries out laws passed by the legislative branch. A veto by the president or state governor can kill the bill, or the veto can be overridden by the legislature, typically with a two-thirds majority vote.

The purpose of the judicial branch is to adjudicate the law. All states have a multilevel judicial system from local courts to the higher courts that decides whether laws and policy are unconstitutional based on that state's constitution. Decisions can vary from state to state. For example, in Michigan the state Supreme Court ruled in the 1960s that "free public school education" means that textbooks and other school supplies must be provided to students. Courts in other states have made different rulings based on exactly the same constitutional language.

In the federal government, the U.S. Supreme Court has broad discretion as to whether it will hear a case or not. When it accepts a case and makes a decision, the court rules whether something is constitutional or unconstitutional—whether or not it is permitted under the U.S. Constitution. The Supreme Court usually hears cases on appeal from lower federal courts or from courts in the states.

How a Bill Becomes a Law

The following figure shows the basics of how a bill becomes a law. As shown in the figure, a bill must follow a legislative process: introduction by a member, assigned to a committee for study, released for a vote, and moved to the other house. It is then sent to another committee and follows the same

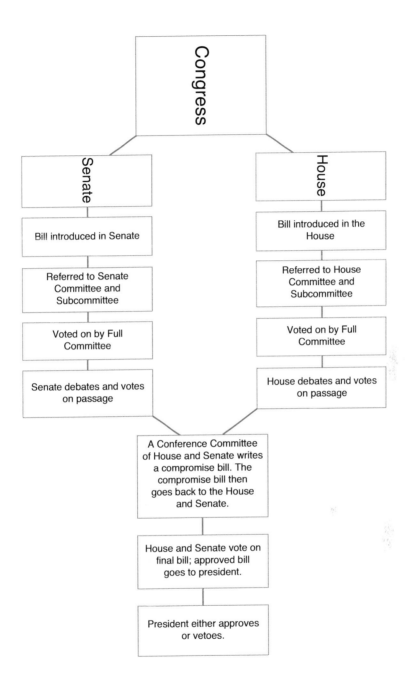

procedure. Approval moves the bill to the president (or governor), where the bill may be signed or vetoed. If a presidential or governor's veto has been overridden, the bill becomes a law. Although most states follow this same procedure, some states do so with individual modifications. In both state and federal legislatures, members sometimes use parliamentary procedures to

Working with Governance ◆ 137

stall passage or to substitute language, sometimes changing the entire meaning of the bill.

Where Do I Begin?

An advocate's starting point is to determine who has jurisdiction over a current issue. Is it a local issue, state, or national issue? Once you have determined the jurisdiction issue, you next need to determine the branch issue. Is this an issue that should be considered by the executive, legislative, or judicial branch? The function of the legislative branch is to make the law, the executive branch to administer the law, and the judicial branch to adjudicate the law. But the roles are often blurred, and the adoption of rules and regulations, which occurs in the executive branch, is similar to the legislative process. The following form presents a simple way to clarify issues and the related branch.

Jurisdiction	Action to Take
Federal	
State	
Local	
Branch	**Action to Take**
Executive	
Legislative	
Judicial	

What Does Governance Mean to Me as an Advocate?

Advocacy efforts are essential at all levels. There are movers and shakers from your local community all the way up to Washington on all education issues. (Chapter X: X Factor: Pitfalls to Avoid goes into depth on defining the movers and shakers.) Generally the closer decision making is to you as an advocate, the more likely you are to be successful in impacting the decision. On the other hand, an advocate needs to make sure legislators know the bill's impact on local students, schools, and communities. Knowledge of the governance process and knowing the appropriate actions to take are keys to successful advocacy. Many school leaders regularly visit their state capital to talk with their legislator or the staff responsible for dealing with educational issues.

Final Thoughts

One aspect of advocacy is working with your local, state, and national governance groups. Understanding each group and how each group works is critical should you want to be a successful advocate.

Final Reflection Questions

What challenge do you face in this particular area of advocacy?
What was the most important thing you learned in this chapter?
How can you apply that lesson in your own situation?
In six months, if you look back on this learning, what would you like to have accomplished?

X

X Factor: Pitfalls to Avoid

Good things do not come easy. The road is lined with pitfalls.

—Desi Arnaz

Throughout the book, we've focused on effective strategies for advocacy. In this chapter, we'll shift our attention to the pitfalls that can hinder your efforts. There are eight pitfalls in advocacy.

Eight Pitfalls of Advocacy

1. Being unprepared
2. Blurring the issue
3. Not knowing the rules
4. Pushing too hard
5. Using derogatory language
6. Forgetting to ask the question
7. Taking it personally
8. Burning bridges

Being Unprepared

The lack of preparation is a major pitfall. You simply cannot be too prepared when advocating. Preparation includes considering every possible outcome of the desired position, whether positive or negative. You want to be able to answer any question a potential supporter might ask. We spoke with one principal who wanted to try a new program in his school. All his teachers were on board, as were many parents. However, when he approached his district-level supervisor about the change, he found out he was unprepared. She asked him questions about the long-term impact, both financially and in terms of student achievement. He had data about the initial implementation, but he could not provide a three-year projection, which was what she needed to be able to support his recommendation. It's important to be *over*prepared.

Blurring the Issue

A second pitfall is blurring your issue. We recommend a laser-like focus on your advocacy efforts, in order to have the best chance for success. Too often, we are taken off track, and when that happens, you lose support for your issue. In another case, a superintendent was advocating for a change in the starting and ending times for elementary schools, so that young children were not waiting for a bus too early in the morning. By beginning the elementary day later, the same buses that transported middle/high school buses could pick up elementary students rather than running separate buses. This could result in significant financial savings that could be redirected to instructional programs. From her perspective, there were only benefits to the change.

She met with principals to share her plan. Although they were interested, they quickly began to ask questions on related issues, such as the sleep patterns of high school students, whether the pay for bus drivers should be increased, and whether video cameras and seat belts should be on the buses. By the end of the meeting, she did not have the support of principals, mainly because they became distracted from the issue! Be careful not to be drawn off your message.

Not Knowing the Rules

Another pitfall is not being clear about any rules, spoken or unspoken, that may guide your planning. It's important to understand any guidelines or procedures that need to be followed to share your message.

Sometimes, because we don't understand policies, we make mistakes and are unable to garner support. For example, most districts have explicit guidelines about how things are submitted for budget consideration or for briefing with the Board of Education. Failure to follow the "rules" can undermine your efforts. Almost always, you will want to be sure that your immediate supervisor knows your plans and supports your advocacy efforts.

Pushing Too Hard

Sometimes, despite your best efforts, potential supporters will choose not to support you. Always thank them for their time and move on. Unfortunately, we've met educators who are so passionate about their proposed initiative that they continue to push, which only turns people off. Individual passion can never substitute for building relationships and support for your efforts. Occasionally, the timing may not be right, or the district may be focused on other priorities. That doesn't mean your plans are rejected. They may simply be deferred until another time or a new budget cycle.

Using Derogatory Language

A related issue is using language that is derogatory. Sometimes, this is obvious, such as saying, "I know you probably don't understand what we do in our school, but . . ." Other times, it is subtle, such as, "I appreciate your help, I know it may not make much of a difference, but I do want your support." Watch your wording in your advocacy efforts.

Forgetting to Ask the Question

Occasionally we can share our information effectively but neglect to ask for support. Barbara met with a core teacher and teacher of special needs who wanted to make a change in how they co-taught in the classroom. It wasn't a major change, but they wanted the principal's support, so they scheduled a meeting with him. They explained what they were doing and then shared the research on alternatives, including the one they wanted to use. He was interested and asked a variety of questions. They finished the meeting and left with the impression that he would support the change. Two days later, when he visited the classroom, he was surprised that they had changed what they were doing. There was a breakdown in communication because they never actually told him they were going to try the alternative strategy, and they didn't ask for his support. Don't finish your advocacy efforts without stating clearly what you need.

Taking It Personally

There will be times when, despite your best efforts, a potential backer chooses not to support your position. As we will discuss in the next section, you want to keep the door open for future support. However, especially when we are passionate about an issue, we can be very disappointed with negative responses. It's easy to fall into the trap of taking the rejection personally. Ninety-nine percent of the time, it isn't personal. It is usually something else, such as not having the time to help you, feeling as though it's not important enough to prioritize, holding a different view of the issue, or believing it will have an unexpected impact on something else they support.

Burning Bridges

Finally, don't burn bridges. Again, it's hard when you do your best, design a strong advocacy message and share that message with a potential supporter, and then you don't receive their support. You have invested time and energy, and the results were not what you wanted. A principal once told Barbara, "Nobody remembers what you do. They remember your exit behavior." This is true with your advocacy efforts. It doesn't matter how professionally you acted during the advocacy process if you finish in a negative way. Negative examples include thanking the person for their time in a sarcastic tone, ignoring them after they tell you no, or saying negative things about them to others. These actions will hurt you in the long run. You never know when you will want to come back to this person on another issue. Don't burn bridges.

Final Thoughts

There are pitfalls along your journey to advocacy, and you want to be aware of them in order to avoid them. It's important to be prepared, focus on the issue, know the rules, and ask for support. You'll also want to avoid pushing too hard, using derogatory language, taking rejection personally, and burning bridges. If you avoid these pitfalls, your advocacy efforts will be more successful.

Final Reflection Questions

What challenge do you face in this particular area of advocacy?
What was the most important thing you learned in this chapter?
How can you apply that lesson in your own situation?
In six months, if you look back on this learning, what would you like to have accomplished?

Y

Your Turn

When people talk, listen completely. Most people never listen.

—Ernest Hemingway

Sometimes the tables are turned, and we're the recipient of advocacy. How do you respond? What should you do? There are key principles to follow.

Key Principles

- Be open to the advocate.
- Learn about the issue.
- Do your own homework.
- Talk to your network.
- Don't make a quick decision.
- Resist pressure.
- Be open to a compromise.

Be Open to the Advocate

First, just as you hope others listen to you when you are advocating for an issue, be willing to listen to those talking to you. Find a time, even if it is brief, to meet or talk with them, not allowing other items to interfere. It's important to let them know you are making them a priority, which shows your willingness to listen. What they say may be important to your own issues, and you never know when you may need their support. Look for natural linkages and ways you might be able to partner.

Learn About the Issue

Next, seek to understand the issue. As you listen to their explanation, ask clarifying questions.

Clarifying Questions

> How does this fit into the broader educational system?
>
> How will it impact my school/district?
>
> Does it benefit students? How?
>
> What is the cost factor [material resources]?
>
> What are the nonmaterial costs [time, etc.]?
>
> What are the obstacles to achieving this initiative?
>
> How does it differ from the existing situation?
>
> How does it differ from our current position?

Don't be afraid to ask hard questions and play the devil's advocate. The person is asking you to put your reputation on the line to support their issue. You have to be sure to understand all aspects of it.

Do Your Own Homework

We spoke with one principal who found herself in a tough situation. A school board member proposed changing how funds would be allocated to schools in the district. She met with the school board member, listened, asked a variety of questions, spoke with her leadership team, and decided to support the change. Only after the change was approved did she discover that, by changing this funding, other sets of money would also be impacted, resulting in an overall loss of money for her school.

That's why you always want to do your own homework. Never take what someone else says as the complete truth. Advocates, including you, are going to share information that best supports your issues. We aren't suggesting you mislead or hide information, but other people may. Research the issues, and ask for any data or documentation you might need to make an informed decision.

Talk to Your Network

As a leader, you have a strong network of other leaders who support you, provide input into decision making, and bring another viewpoint to the table. When you are asked to support an issue, it's imperative that you bring this group of people into the process. First, they may see something you don't. For example, a parent may have another perspective, one that informs your decision. Second, if you do support the issue, you have other people who agree with you, so you are not on your own. This is especially helpful if you are supporting something that will directly impact your school. In particular, it can be helpful to seek advice and comment from people who might support as well as resist supporting the issue.

Don't Make a Quick Decision

There are advocates who will pressure you to make a quick decision as to whether to support their issue. Don't! You need time to process their information, as well as gathering your own, in order to fully understand the ramifications for your school or district. You'll also want to consider what type of support you are willing to provide: active or passive.

Examples of Active Support	Examples of Passive Support
■ Talk to a school board member. ■ Allow the advocate access to your stakeholders to share their message. ■ Talk to a parent group. ■ Share information about the issue. ■ Ask your teachers for support. ■ Implement a program.	■ Don't comment on the issue. ■ Take no position on the issue. ■ Remain neutral. ■ Don't interfere with what the advocate is doing.

This is the ultimate question: Are you willing to support the advocate and, if so, how? Be sure you have followed all the steps needed to make the best decision.

Resist Pressure

When you ask for time to make a decision or if you decide not to support an issue, the advocate may pressure you to decide or change your mind. Resist the pressure! It's up to you to control the process. There are a variety of ways to respond when being pressured.

Responding to Pressure

> I need more time.
>
> I need more information.
>
> I need to talk to some other people.
>
> I'm just not ready to make a decision.

Be Open to a Compromise

Sometimes, the best option is to try to compromise with advocates, especially if their issue overlaps with yours. Let's look at an example that North Carolina recently experienced. Generally, educators in the state supported lowering class sizes in the primary grades. This was particularly important because accountability guidelines require that students must be reading on grade level by the end of third grade, and smaller class sizes would assist in meeting that goal.

The state legislature agreed that smaller class size was a good idea, so they decided to mandate them. However, they did not provide additional funding to hire additional teachers. This meant that principals were faced with the decision to replace their art, music, and physical education teachers with general education teachers in order to meet the mandate. Additionally, many school districts were faced with a lack of classroom space, which would require building new classrooms, at an additional cost. Look at how the issues overlap in the figure that follows.

Although both groups wanted smaller class size, the other aspects of education that were impacted had not necessarily been explored. After months of advocacy by educators and other concerned citizens, the legislature passed a new bill that delayed the recommendations for one year in order to give them time to study the issue, including how to fund art, music, and physical education teachers. Some legislators pledged to allocate separate funding for those teachers, but that was not guaranteed.

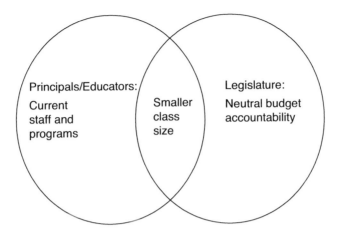

Educators were faced with accepting a compromise: achieving the goal of smaller class sizes and, at least for a year, keeping all existing programs. Legislators also compromised, delaying the plan for a year and keeping the budget neutral for a year, but they also accomplished their goal of accountability by requiring additional reporting by school districts.

Although not ideal for either side, it was a decision that both sides could live with. As one principal told Barbara, "It wasn't the decision we wanted, and it's not ideal, but it's better than what we were dealing with." Sometimes, compromise is the best you can do.

Final Thoughts

Advocacy works both ways. There will be times when someone is advocating for you to support an issue or make a decision. When that happens, it's important to listen, gather information, and carefully choose your position.

Final Reflection Questions

What challenge do you face in this particular area of advocacy?
What was the most important thing you learned in this chapter?
How can you apply that lesson in your own situation?
In six months, if you look back on this learning, what would you like to have accomplished?

Z

Zeroing in on the Essentials

Choose to be an advocate for your school. Or choose not to. That, in itself, is an advocacy decision.

—Unknown

Whether you recognize it or not, every school leader is an advocate. Leaders are always advocating for their school and for the resources and programs to support student learning and improve the educational experience of their students.

Advocacy is one of the most important roles of a school leader. Advocacy includes effectively communicating with the public, as well as with local and state elected officials and the media about your school and about education issues in your community. But advocacy is more than just sharing information. It is also about increasing the capacity of your school community to participate in decisions impacting critical educational issues affecting your students and their school.

In the preceding 25 chapters, we've examined the issue of advocacy and described many of the strategies and tools you may use to be a successful advocate. This chapter will highlight the "essentials" of that discussion and provide a brief overview of advocacy.

Embrace Your Advocacy Role

Advocacy is something leaders do when they talk with a parent about their school's program. Advocacy is something leaders do when they make a presentation at a local service club or organization. Advocacy is something leaders do when they meet with a local school board member or with their state or federal representative. Advocacy is something leaders do when they compose the school newsletter or write a letter to the editor of the local newspaper.

In addition to these roles, advocacy is a way to effectively press for change. It's a way for school leaders to shape and influence policy at all levels and to work with their school community to create a future that will serve students well.

What's critical is that leaders recognize that they are advocates. The things they say, the stories they share, the memos they write, and the presentations they make are all a form of advocacy and have the potential to shape the programs and resources at their school.

Build a Network

Skillful leaders and skillful advocates recognize the benefit of building coalitions and networks of support. In Chapter N: Networking, we shared specific strategies for building a network or coalition. But the most successful advocates are those who understand the value of having a team of people they can rely on to offer advice and support and who can also help to both share and gather information.

Perhaps the most critical part of a network is to recognize the value of including people with a variety of perspectives and points of view. Including only known supporters is detrimental to your success. Their advice may make you feel good, but they probably won't alert you to concerns about issues you're discussing. So always be sure your network includes people with whom you may not always agree. After all, you'll hear from dissenters eventually, and it can be very helpful to understand their perspectives early so that you can respond effectively.

Pay Attention to Relationships

As with most things, the quality of the relationship you have with others can shape the impact of your advocacy efforts. Every school, like every organization, is comprised of a variety of stakeholders. Those groups will include supporters as well as those who are less supportive of your school and your efforts.

Complicating matters even more, a person or stakeholder group may be supportive on one issue and resistant on another. What's critical is that you recognize the importance of listening to every voice, every point of view, treating each group respectfully, and diligently identifying any issues that emerge. Resisters may well be supporters on some other issue, or you may be able to provide information that will help them become more supportive.

Be Clear About Vision

If one theme is consistent for school leaders, it is the importance of vision, both personal vision and shared vision. That's also true for your advocacy efforts. In Chapter V: Vision: Personal and Shared, we discussed the importance of vision and provided a model for developing both a personal vision and a shared vision.

Your personal vision consists of your most fundamental beliefs about your work, your relationships, and your life. Those beliefs shape everything you do, including your work as an advocate. For example, if you believe people are trustworthy, you will respond one way. But if you think them untrustworthy, you will respond differently.

While holding a personal vision is important, the most successful leaders and most successful advocates are those who recognize how important it is to work with stakeholders to build a shared vision, one developed collaboratively with others and one that is widely embraced and supported.

Vision is critical because it guides your advocacy efforts. Everything you do, every message you craft, every discussion you hold, and every person you contact has the potential to support your vision. Your advocacy for your school and for your students is essential.

Expand Your Capacity with Technology

In Chapters E: Engaging Through Technology and K: Keys to Social Media, we discussed various forms of technology and how they can enhance your advocacy efforts. We won't repeat ourselves here other than to remind you that technology is an efficient, cost-effective means to share information with a large group of people.

Like it or not, social media has become an indispensable tool for advocacy. It's a powerful way to shape your message, to share information, and to connect with stakeholders and key decision makers. Be attentive to your school's presence online. Don't neglect it, and don't abandon it. Technology, especially social media, has become the most common way to share information and to learn what others are thinking. Make sure your school's website and social media accounts are active, updated regularly, attractive, and helpful to stakeholders.

When we discussed future trends, we also talked about technology. One thing we're really confident about is that technology will continue to evolve and become even more imbedded in everyday life. So monitor those trends. Learn about new social media tools, and stay current on how to use technology to expand your capacity as an advocate.

Develop a Toolkit

The most successful advocates recognize that there are lots of different tools to be used for advocacy. They also recognize that every tool doesn't fit every issue or situation. And all tools don't have the same impact on every stakeholder.

So effective advocates develop and use a whole set of tools that they can use. Think of it this way. Every skilled advocate has a big toolbox with a variety of tools. For every task, they select the tool that's most appropriate to accomplishing the task.

Let's highlight a few of the tools included in this book:

- In Chapter N: Networking, there is a description of how to create a network, a key communicator network.
- Chapter E: Engaging Through Technology provides strategies for improving your school's website and keeping content fresh.
- A model for designing an Elevator Talk or writing a One-Page Fact Sheet is included in Chapter F: Framing Your Message.
- A sample template for developing an advocacy plan is included in Chapter D: Designing an Advocacy Plan, along with a sample plan.
- Tools for developing a social media presence are included in Chapter K: Keys to Social Media.
- Templates for creating a personal vision and a shared vision are provided in Chapter V: Vision: Personal and Shared.
- Steps for developing a public relations campaign are included in Chapter P: Public Relations 101.
- Strategies for responding to resistance are included in Chapter R: Resistance to Change.
- Tips for avoiding pitfalls are included in Chapter X: X Factor: Pitfalls to Avoid.

Final Thoughts

Each and every one of us is an advocate. Everything we do has the potential to build support for our school and its programs. Whether leaders embrace their advocacy role or not, their work and their actions reflect on your school and can either build or lessen support.

Throughout this book, we've focused on the broad ideas and concepts that are part of advocacy. We've also provided some strategies and tools that can be used to refine and enhance your work as an advocate.

Embrace your role as an advocate and recognize the power of advocacy to transform your work as a school leader and to strengthen and refine your school.

Final Reflection Questions

What challenge do you face in this particular area of advocacy?

What was the most important thing you learned in this chapter?

How can you apply that lesson in your own situation?

In six months, if you look back on this learning, what would you like to have accomplished?

Bibliography

Books

Buber, P. (2011). *Tell to win*. New York: Crown Business.

Buck, F. (2015). *Get organized: Time management for school leaders*. New York: Routledge.

Daley, J. (2011). *Advocacy championing: Ideas and influencing others*. New Haven, CT: Yale University Press.

Denning, S. (2011). *The leader's guide to storytelling*. Hoboken, NJ: John Wiley & Sons.

Dinkmeyer, D., & Losoncy, L. E. (1980). The encouragement book: Becoming a positive person. Englewood Cliffs, NJ: Prentice-Hall.

Gladwell, M. (2002). *The tipping point: How little things can make a big difference*. New York: Little, Brown and Company.

Guilfoyle, K. (2015). *Making the case: How to be your own best advocate*. New York: Harper.

Heath, C., & Heath, D. (2010). *Switch: How to change things when change is hard*. New York: Crown Business.

Heinrichs, J. (2013). *Thank you for arguing: What Aristotle, Lincoln, and Homer Simpson can teach us about the art of persuasion* (2nd edition). New York: Three Rivers Press.

Kotter, J. P., & Whitehead, L. A. (2010). *Buy-In: Saving your idea from getting shot down*. Cambridge, MA: Harvard Business Press.

Kush, C. (2004). *The one-hour activist*. San Francisco: Jossey-Bass.

Marx, G. (2006). *Sixteen trends, their profound impact on our future: Implications for students, education, communities and the whole of society*. Alexandria, VA: Educational Research Service.

Maslow, A. H. (1968). *Toward a psychology of being*. New York: Van Nostrand.

Millman, N., Chernoff, C., & Hammer, J. (2015). *Advocating creatively: Stories of contemporary social change pioneers*. North Charleston, SC: CreateSpace Independent Publishing Platform.

Phillips, B. (2013). *The media training bible*. Washington, DC: SpeakGood Press.

Porterfield, K., & Carnes, M. (2008). *Why school communication matters: Strategies from PR professionals.* East Greenbush, NY: R&L Education.

Rettberg, J. (2008). *Blogging.* Cambridge: Polity Press.

Seiter, M. (1983). *Shaping the body politic: Legislative training for the physical educator.* Springfield, MA: American Association for Health, Physical Education, and Recreation.

Shaw, R. (2013). *The activist's handbook: Winning social change in the 21st century* (2nd edition). Oakland: University of California Press.

Simmons, A. (2006). *The story factor.* New York: Basic Books.

Simmons, A. (2007). *Whoever tells the best story wins.* New York: American Management Association.

Unsicker, J. (2013). *Confronting power: The practice of policy advocacy.* Sterling, VA: Kumarian Press.

Williamson, R., & Blackburn, B. (2016). *The principalship from A to Z* (2nd edition). New York: Routledge.

Williamson, R., & Blackburn, B. (2017). *Rigor in your classroom: A toolkit for leaders* (2nd edition). New York: Routledge.

Williamson, R., & Johnston, J. H. (2012). *The school leader's guide to social media.* New York: Routledge Education.

Other Resources

American Heart Association. (n.d.). *You're the cure: The 60 second advocate: How to guide.*

American Heart Association. (2004). *People with heart: Saving lives through information, advocacy and action.* Heart and Stroke Lobby Day.

American Heart Association. (2008). *You're the cure: North Carolina regional team advocacy manual.*

American Heart Association. (2010). *You're the cure: North Carolina regional team advocacy manual.*

American Public Health Association. (1999). *Advocates' handbook: A guide for effective public health advocacy.*

American Public Health Association. (2010). *PHACT campaign toolkit.*

American Public Health Association. (2011). *PHACT campaign toolkit.*

Association of North Carolina Boards of Health (2001). *Advocating for the public's health: A training manual.* Conference Proceedings.

Changing Minds. (n.d.). "Three-stage negotiation." http://changingminds.org/disciplines/negotiation/three-stage/three-stage.htm

Haughey, D. (2014). "A Brief History of SMART Goals." www.projectsmart.co.uk/brief-history-of-smart-goals.php

Intel Corporation. (2010). *Intel social media guidelines*. Retrieved August 5, 2017, from www.intel.com/content/www/us/en/legal/intel-social-media-guidelines.html

Kelchner, L. (n.d.). "Top Ten effective negotiation skills." Chron. http://smallbusiness.chron.com/top-ten-effective-negotiation-skills-31534.html

Lenhart, A. (2015). *Teens, social media & technology overview 2015*. Retrieved August 05, 2017, from www.pewinternet.org/2015/04/09/teens-social-media-technology-2015/

Mountain Area Health Education Center. (2006). *Building local support for public health*. Conference Proceedings.

North Carolina Association of County Commissioners. (2012). *Legislative goals handbook*. www.ncacc.org/147/Legislative-Goals

Parent-Teacher Association. *National PTA advocacy toolkit*. Retrieved August 17, 2016 from www.pta.org/AdvocacyToolkit

Porterfield, K., & Carnes, M. (2010). *10 reasons you should pay attention to social media*. Retrieved December 16, 2010, from www.aasa.org

Showalter, A. (n.d.). *Beyond fundraisers and fly-ins: 105 ways to keep in touch with your elected officials all year*. Poughkeepsie, NY: American Heart Association.

Skillsyouneed.com. (n.d.). "What is negotiation?" https://www.skillsyouneed.com/ips/negotiation.html

Society of Health and Physical Educators. (2017). *State advocacy toolkit*.

Spangler, B. (2003). "Coalition Building." Beyond Intractability. www.beyondintractability.org/essay/coalition-building

Appendix

Recommended Education Advocacy Websites

American Public Health Association
www.apha.org/legislative

Association for Supervision and Curriculum Development
www.ascd.org/public-policy.aspx

Council of Chief State School Officers
www.ccsso.org/What_We_Do/Legislation_and_Advocacy.html

National Association of Elementary School Principals
www.naesp.org/advocacy

National Association of Secondary School Principals
www.nassp.org/advocacy

National Education Association
http://edadvocacy.nea.org

National Parent Teacher Association
www.pta.org/AdvocacyToolkit

National School Boards Association
www.nsba.org/advocacy

Network for Public Education
https://networkforpubliceducation.org

The School Superintendents' Association
www.aasa.org/Content.aspx?id=854

SHAPE America (Health and Physical Education)
www.aahperd.org/advocacy

Stand for Children
http://stand.org/national/about

Taylor & Francis eBooks

Helping you to choose the right eBooks for your Library

Add Routledge titles to your library's digital collection today. Taylor and Francis ebooks contains over 50,000 titles in the Humanities, Social Sciences, Behavioural Sciences, Built Environment and Law.

Choose from a range of subject packages or create your own!

Benefits for you
- Free MARC records
- COUNTER-compliant usage statistics
- Flexible purchase and pricing options
- All titles DRM-free.

Benefits for your user
- Off-site, anytime access via Athens or referring URL
- Print or copy pages or chapters
- Full content search
- Bookmark, highlight and annotate text
- Access to thousands of pages of quality research at the click of a button.

Free Trials Available
We offer free trials to qualifying academic, corporate and government customers.

eCollections – Choose from over 30 subject eCollections, including:

Archaeology	Language Learning
Architecture	Law
Asian Studies	Literature
Business & Management	Media & Communication
Classical Studies	Middle East Studies
Construction	Music
Creative & Media Arts	Philosophy
Criminology & Criminal Justice	Planning
Economics	Politics
Education	Psychology & Mental Health
Energy	Religion
Engineering	Security
English Language & Linguistics	Social Work
Environment & Sustainability	Sociology
Geography	Sport
Health Studies	Theatre & Performance
History	Tourism, Hospitality & Events

For more information, pricing enquiries or to order a free trial, please contact your local sales team:
www.tandfebooks.com/page/sales

 The home of Routledge books

www.tandfebooks.com